AF608088

The Catholic University of America
Canon Law Studies
No. 305

THE USE OF THE PORTABLE ALTAR

A Historical Synopsis and a Commentary

BY

Reverend Thomas J. Welsh, J.C.L.

PRIEST OF THE ARCHDIOCESE OF PHILADELPHIA

A DISSERTATION

Submitted to the Faculty of the School of Canon Law of the Catholic University of America in Partial Fulfillment of the Requirements for the Degree of Doctor of Canon Law

THE CATHOLIC UNIVERSITY OF AMERICA PRESS
WASHINGTON, D. C.
1950

Nihil Obstat:
CLEMENT V. BASTNAGEL, J.U.D.
Censor Deputatus
Washingtonii, D. C., die 31 augusti, 1950

Imprimatur:
✠ D. CARD. DOUGHERTY
Archiepiscopus Philadelphiensis
Philadelphiae, die 2 septembris 1950

MURRAY & HEISTER—WASHINGTON, D. C.
PRINTED IN THE UNITED STATES OF AMERICA

To MY MOTHER
and the Memory of MY FATHER

TABLE OF CONTENTS

FOREWORD

In the present Code of Canon Law, as well as in canonical legislation in the past, the institute of the portable altar occupies a somewhat unique position in that its use generally presupposes some unusual circumstance. This is not to be regarded as strange, since it has ever been the tendency in the Church to surround the celebration of Holy Mass with all the dignity, ceremony and splendor that its august nature demands.

If the places in Palestine, hallowed by the footprints of Christ, have been sought and secured as Christian shrines at the price of much Christian blood, is it any wonder that the places in which Christ in the Blessed Sacrament has been present should also be set apart from worldly pursuits? Since the Christians wrested recognition from the Roman Empire, places have been set apart and hallowed again and again by repeated reenactments of the Holy Sacrifice of the Mass. Christ in the Eucharist, just as Christ in the flesh, sanctifies the spot.

If one keeps this in mind, it is clear that the position of the portable altar in law and in the liturgy will always be one that is out of the ordinary, since the use of the portable altar stands adverse to the natural tendency to sanctify and hallow the spot wherein Mass is said.

The purpose of this dissertation will be to trace the history and the present law on the institute of the portable altar, with a view specifically to those matters in which its use differs from the accustomed mode of things. This will be especially true in the element of privilege involved in the use of the portable altar, and in the question of the relationship of the portable altar to the precept of hearing Mass, since the law in the Code regarding the place for the fulfilling of the Mass precept does not treat expressly of the portable altar.

The writer wishes to express his gratitude to His Eminence, Dennis Cardinal Dougherty, Archbishop of Philadelphia, for the opportunity to pursue advanced studies in Canon Law; to the Faculty of the School of Canon Law at the Catholic University of America for their kind guidance and assistance; and to all others who have aided in any way in making the completion of this work possible.

INTRODUCTION

The topic of the portable altar in its historical aspects includes a treatment of its origin and development in the perspective not only of legislation but also of the liturgy. Since the liturgical factors in their historical aspects have already been treated in a Canon Law Dissertation,[1] and also at length in other works,[2] the present work proposes to treat of the legislative elements in their historical perspective as they touch the use of the portable altar.

The following historical conspectus deals initially with the use of the portable altar as it was provided for either by law or by custom. The chief consideration, however, will center upon the use of this altar as deriving through the privileges which were granted at a later time either in the law itself or by way of pontifical indult.

---

[1] Bliley, *Altars According to the Code of Canon Law,* The Catholic University of America Canon Law Studies, n. 38 (Washington, D. C.: The Catholic University of America, 1927).

[2] Braun, *Der christliche Altar in seiner geschictlichen Entwicklung* (2 vols., Muenchen,: Alte Meister Guenther Koch & Co., 1924); Henny, *Der Altar im kanonischen Recht* (Romae: Pontificia Universitas Gregoriana, 1940).

PART ONE:

LEGISLATION PRIOR TO THE COUNCIL OF TRENT

CHAPTER I

EARLIEST LEGISLATIVE REFERENCES

The history of the portable altar is naturally very closely connected with the history of the Mass itself, and the development of the one is in many particulars parallel to the other. Just as in other liturgical matters that have their beginnings in uncertain history the authors are not in complete agreement, so the authors differ too in tracing the origin of the portable altar as it is known today. One school of thought insists that no trace can be found before the eighth century, while the opposition professes to find proof that the portable altar must have been used by the Apostles themselves.

When one examines the historical data that have so far been uncovered, the first direct reference to the portable altar is found in a letter of about the year 511, written by Bishops Licinius of Tours, Eustachius of Angers, and Melanius of Rennes, to the missionary priests Lovocal and Catihern, who had been sent from England to labor in Brittany. Reports had reached the bishops that the priests were saying Mass in the houses of the Bretons on consecrated tables. In their letter the bishops ordered them to desist from the practice at once.[1] It is interesting to note here in view of the later developments regarding the portable altar that this first real and direct mention was by way of a curb on its use. This is indeed a suitable keynote for the history of the institute.

There can be little doubt that the letter referred to above spoke of portable altars when it mentioned " consecrated tables." This becomes more evident if it is borne in mind that the two priests were missionaries in a pagan land. Under such circumstances

---

[1] Amort, *Elementa Juris Canonici Veteris et Moderni* (3 vols., Ferrariae, 1763), I, 353-4. In the preface to Part II of Vol. I the author states that the letter is from the manuscript Code, *Canonica Diessensis,* of the eighth century. Cf. Many, *De Missa* (Parisiis, 1903), p. 5; Braun, *Der christliche Altar,* I, 74.

there could surely be no permanent churches or altars, and accordingly the mention of a " consecrated table " seems definitely to point to a portable altar.

With this as a starting point one comes face to face with the arguments of those who claim that the portable altar had an even earlier origin. The leader of this school of thought is Gattico (1704–1754).[2] In his monumental work this author has taken the lead in the field, and he still retains it despite progress in research relative to the development in the law. His argument follows the line that in the history of the early Church there exist many references which point to the saying of Mass in the fields, in prisons, in homes, and in many other places in which it was impossible to have a permanent altar. This argument rests for its force on the assumption that an altar was required then as now for the saying of every Mass. Thus, if no permanent altar was possible, then some sort of portable one had to be used.

" Just as no religion has ever existed without a sacrifice, so no sacrifice has ever existed without an altar." It is with these words that Martène (1654–1739) began his discussion of the altar and sacred vessels of Christian antiquity.[3]

Since an altar, i.e. a table for the sacrifice, was to be considered in the very nature of the Mass as a repetition of the Last Supper, Martène took for granted the universal Christian use of an altar, and thereupon proceeded rather to the discussion of whether the Apostles used a wooden or a stone altar. In connection with this discussion he referred to the fragments of a wooden altar now preserved in the church of St. Praxedes in Rome. According to a well-founded and ancient tradition these fragments constitute the remains of an altar that St. Peter used in the house of Pudens, a Roman senator. It is also said to have been used by later popes in the catacombs.[4] Whether or not there is truth in these tra-

---

[2] *De Oratoriis Domesticis et de Usu Altaris Portatilis* (Romae, 1746), cap. I, nn. 10, 11 (hereafter cited as Gattico).

[3] *De Antiquis Ecclesiae Ritibus* (3 vols., Rotomagi, 1700–1702), lib. III, pars I, cap. III, art. 6 (hereafter cited as Martène).

[4] Martène, *ibid.*, art. 6, n. 2. Cf. Gattico, cap. I, n. 4, who however stated that the altar is rather to be found in a chapel of the church of St. Pudentiana. Hassett (" Altar," *Catholic Encyclopedia* [15 vols., Index and 2

ditions, they still serve the practical purpose of showing the early belief in the use and even necessity of altars for Mass.

Of weight in this discussion is the opinion of Pope Benedict XIV (1740–1758). Answering the objections raised by the early heretics, such as Celsus and Caecilius of the second century,[5] that the Christians had no images, temples or altars, he admitted that they had nothing that compared with the temples of the pagans, but that they certainly did have altars that could be moved from place to place, not only for convenience but also for protection in time of persecution. Continuing the discussion he recalled the account given by Philostorgius (368–ca. 425) concerning St. Lucian, priest and martyr of Antioch who died in 312, that, when chained in prison so that he could not rise, he said Mass reclining on his back and using his breast for an altar.[6] Lastly he adverted to the case of Theodoret, Bishop of Cyrrhus in Syria (ca. 423–457), who when asked by the dying hermit, Maris, said Mass in his cell on the hands of deacons as an altar.[7] Summing up what he had said, the Pope concluded that these two cases are worthy more of our admiration than of our imitation, since " it has always been the constant and perpetual practice of the Church that Mass should be celebrated on an altar." [8]

Speaking on this point and about these very same cases, Gasparri (1852–1934) [9] regarded them as extremely exceptional cases,

---

Supplements, New York, 1907–1922], I, 362) stated that there are, now, one in the church of St. John Lateran, and another in the church of St. Pudentiana. The tradition is merely local, and the evidence seems unconvincing. Thalhofer (*Handbuch der katholichen Liturgik* [2 vols., Freiburg im Breisgau, 1883–1893], I, 754) mentioned simply the one in the church of St. John Lateran, without passing judgment regarding its history.

[5] Cf. Origen, *Contra Celsum,* lib. VIII, nn. 16, 17—Migne, *Patrologiae Cursus Completus, Series Graeca* (161 vols. in 164, Parisiis, 1856–1866), III, 754–755 (hereafter cited as *MPG*); Arnobius, *Adversus Gentes,* lib. VI, cap. 1 sqq.—Migne, *Patrologiae Cursus Completus, Series Latina* (221 vols., Parisiis, 1844–1864), V, 1162 (hereafter cited as *MPL*).

[6] Philostorgius, *Ecclesiastica Historia,* lib. II, cap. 13.—*MPG,* LXV, 476.

[7] *Historia Religiosa,* cap. 20.—*MPG,* LXXXII, 1429.

[8] Benedictus XIV, *De Sacrosancto Missae Sacrificio* (3 vols., Prati, 1843), lib. I, cap. II, n. 4.

[9] *Tractatus Canonicus de Sanctissima Eucharistia* (2 vols., Parisiis, 1897), I, 311.

warranted only in absolute necessity, and hence related as quite remarkable occurrences. The abiding tradition, as evincing the early and constant use of altars in the Church, and as reflecting the established notions of people everywhere that an altar is essential to every religion, invites at least the assumption, if it does not also furnish convincing proof, that altars have always been deemed a prerequisite for the offering of the sacrifice of holy Mass.

In the light of this premise the weight of the indirect references to the early use of the portable altar can be felt. For, once it is admitted that an altar of some sort was essential for the sacrificial offering of the Mass, then it follows that in very many instances the only possible altar under the given circumstances was a portable altar of some sort.

In the light of that thought a very casual look at the history of the early Church, even apart from any actual documentary proof, should convince anyone of the necessity of portable altars from the very beginning. That conclusion is reached in view of the almost continual persecutions that the Church suffered, first from the Jews, and then from the Romans, until the Emperor Constantine issued the Edict of Milan in 313. It appears likely that the example of St. Paul, who according to the narrative of the *Acts of the Apostles* offered Mass in the upper chamber of a house in Troas after he had discoursed to the people, was followed in the Church until such time that the Church enjoyed at least a tacit recognition from the State. This seems substantiated by a statement of Dionysius, Archbishop of Alexandria (ca. 247–ca. 265), around the year 255, when he related [10] that amid widespread and intense persecution, which made death imminent for the Christians, the feasts were nevertheless joyfully celebrated by them. Every place where affliction beset them—the open field, the desert solitude, the storm-tossed ship, the wayfarer's inn, even the prison itself—became a place for the sacred assembly in their manifestation of holy zeal. The "*sacer conventus*" was their gathering together at the celebration of Mass.

When during the persecutions in Africa the churches had been

[10] Eusebius, *Historia Ecclesiastica,* lib. VII, cap. 22.—*MPG,* XX, 688.

destroyed, the Divine Mysteries were celebrated wherever possible.[11] Also in the military camps of Constantine, the first Christian emperor, there was a tent erected in the form of a church. There occurs mention of the soldiers' participation in the Divine Mysteries, so there could well have been need of a portable altar. This seems especially likely because of the need to move the camp from place to place, often in great haste. It is also reported that the sons of Constantine continued this very praiseworthy practice, as did the later emperors.[12]

Regarding the use of altars in prisons, in addition to the exceptional cases involving St. Lucian (+ 312) and Theodoret of Cyrrhus (+ 457), there is an interesting account in Gattico, namely,[13] that St. Dionysius of Paris (third century) had a portable altar which he is said to have used while he was in prison. Also during the persecution under Emperor Gallus (251–253) St. Cyprian warned his priests and deacons that they should be cautious when going to the prisons to offer Mass there for the confessors of the faith.[14]

Apparently the chief reason why Mass was said in private homes was the presence of some sick person who otherwise would have been deprived of the consolation of the Holy Sacrifice. St. Augustine (354–430) related that Mass was offered in the house of a certain Hesperius by permission of the bishop with a view to dispelling the harm which had befallen the family, the servants and the animals through being haunted by spirits.[15] Of St. Paulinus, Bishop of Nola (409–431), it is related that, when he knew his

---

[11] Victor Vitensis, *Epistolae,* lib. I, cap. 5.—*MPL,* LVIII, 188.

[12] Sozomen, *Historia Ecclesiastica,* lib. I, cap. 8.—*MPG,* LXVII, 880. The text reads: "Quoties ad bellum proficisceretur tabernaculum ad Ecclesiae similitudinem fabricatum circumferre consueverat, ita ut ne quidem in solitudine constitutus tam Ipse, quam Exercitus ejus Sacra Aede careret in qua Deum laudare, ac preces fundere, et Sacra Mysteria percipere possent. Sequebantur enim Sacerdotes et Diaconi tabernaculo assidentes, qui juxta Ecclesiae ritum ejusmodi officia obirent." The text is self-explanatory. For a more detailed discussion of it, cf. Gattico, cap. V, nn. 1, 2.

[13] *De Oratoriis Domesticis et de Usu Altaris Portatilis,* cap. I, n. 8.

[14] S. Cyprianus, *Epistola IV,* nn. 1, 2.—*MPL,* IV, 230.

[15] *De Civitate Dei,* lib. XXII, cap. 8.—*Corpus Scriptorum Ecclesiasticorum Latinorum* (Viennae, 1866–), XI, Pars II, 602.

last days were upon him, he said Mass one day at his bedside with the assistance of the visiting bishops, Symmachus and Acindymus.[16]

Some of the old sacramentaries provided special formulas for the Masses to be said in the homes of the sick. Martène, for instance,[17] referred to the *Liber Sacramentorum* of the Monastery of Moissac, which dates from the year 800. It contains a *Missa pro Infirmo,* which was clearly intended for the home in view of the wording of the Collect, "*in hac domo.*" Similar expressions occurred in the prayers "*Super oblata*" and "*Infra actionem.*"

These examples reflect evidence that in consequence of the unfavorable reception which the pagan world accorded to the Church from its very origin, the Church could not securely establish and maintain public edifices which through their dedication to divine worship were to serve that exclusive purpose. Rather, it remained for the Church to foster the religious life, to instruct the faithful, to confer on them the sacraments, and to offer the sacrifice of the Mass under whatever temporal and local circumstances it became possible to do so. This state of affairs, attended as it was with the belief that the altar was essential for the act of sacrifice, could well occasion a rather general use of portable altars, at least until the end of the great persecutions. If such was the actual state of things, what argument is employed by those who claim that there is no indication of the existence of the portable altar before the eighth century?

In treating of this controversy Van-Espen (1646–1728)[18] pointed to Thiers (1636–1706) and Thomassin (1619–1695) as having taught the eighth-century origin of the portable altar. However a search in the writings of Thomassin has not uncovered any warrant for this assertion.[19] This author listed two causes which, as he thought, gave rise to the use of sacred stones that could, when they had been blessed by the bishop, serve the purpose

---

[16] *Epistola de Obitu S. Paulini*, n. 2.—*MPL,* LIII, 860.

[17] *De Antiquis Ecclesiae Ritibus,* lib. I, pars VII, art. 4, Ordo IX.

[18] *Jus Ecclesiasticum Universum* (4 vols., Lovanii, 1778), Pars II, sectio I, tit. V, cap. 8, n. 10.

[19] Cf. *Vetus et Nova Ecclesiae Disciplina circa Beneficia et Beneficiarios* (10 vols., Magontiaci, 1787), *De Beneficiis,* Pars I, lib. II, cap. 25, nn. 2, 3.

of altars. The first of these causes was the consideration that the lack of an altar or something to take its place would have made it impossible for the pious to enjoy the privilege of benefiting from the celebration of Mass whenever they undertook a lengthy journey. The second was the fact that it frequently proved necessary to celebrate the Sacred Mysteries in a chapel or in a domestic oratory which did not warrant the permanent status of a solemn dedication. There was also to be taken into account the fact that bishops could not possibly undertake throughout all their territory to bless every little chapel. As a result, lest Mass would have to be offered in a totally unconsecrated place, the bishops attached a blessing to stones whose convenient size allowed them to be transferred from place to place as the need arose.

Now, just as these arguments certainly point to the need of a portable altar during the eighth century, so they likewise serve to show the existence of a similar need even in earlier times. Thomassin nowhere attempted to use them to demonstrate that the eighth century was the earliest possible time for the appearance of such altars. In fact, when he referred to canon 47 of the Council of Paris (829), he indicated that the portable altar had already been in frequent use for a long time. Thus it appears that his statement points rather to an early use of the portable altar. So Van-Espen appears to have drawn too sweeping a conclusion when he represented Thomassin as implying that the eighth century marked the origin of the use of the portable altar.

Van-Espen sought further to substantiate his claim through an appeal to the arguments presented by Thiers,[20] who recalled the cases of St. Lucian (+ 312) and of Theodoret of Cyrrhus (+ ca. 457), the former having offered the sacrifice of the Mass on his own breast, and the latter having done so by utilizing the hands of his deacons. From the narrative of these two cases Thiers concluded that, if portable altars had then been in use, they would most certainly have been employed. However, to this argument one may well reply that these cases in all likelihood reflect, not what then was the normal usage, but what then as at any other time constituted an extraordinary procedure. It seems

[20] Cf. *Dissértation ecclésiastique sur les principaux autels des églises, les jubés des églises, la clôture des choers des églises* (Paris, 1688), cap. 2.

much more defensible to assume that these cases were recounted in view of the quite exceptional procedure which they implied, so that the usual manner in the offering of the sacrifice of the Mass relied on the use of a consecrated stone, i.e., of a portable altar.

Relative to the counterarguments which point to the existence of the portable altar in the early days of the Church, Thiers did not offer any rebuttal. Gattico [21] pointed out that Thiers was well aware of the still extant altar of St. Peter, and that his failure to acknowledge that fact was in itself enough to challenge the tenableness of his opinion. Thiers likewise failed to take into account the letter which the three Bishops of Angers, Rennes and Tours wrote to the missionaries in Brittany around the year 511. It is of course possible that the fact of this letter had not come to the knowledge of Thiers.

In view of the positive evidence that exists in the matter, and in the light of the more acceptable logic that attends the assumption that altar and sacrifice have always been related concepts in the Church, there is a very strong likelihood that the portable altar was in use in the very early days of the Church, and even in a rather widespread manner during the times of persecution. This is the position which was held by Gattico, and it is also the one which was defended by Bliley (1893–1943).[22]

Bona (1609–1674), in pointing to a text taken from the writings of Venerable Bede (673–735), which text will receive a special consideration later in this study, singled it out as furnishing proof that the portable altar had a very ancient beginning.[23] Braun (1857–1947) dealt with the question at greater length, and argued along the same lines as Gattico.[24] Thalhofer (1825–1891) and Eisenhofer (+ 1942), while not going into the point thoroughly, likewise referred to Venerable Bede's text, and argued therefrom for the certain existence of the portable altar at least in the seventh century.[25]

---

[21] *De Oratoriis Domesticis et de Usu Altaris Portatilis,* cap. I, n. 2.

[22] *Altars According to the Code of Canon Law,* p. 43.

[23] *Rerum Liturgicarum Libri Duo* (Romae, 1671), lib. I, cap. XX, n. 2.

[24] *Der christliche Altar,* I, 73.

[25] *Handbuch der katholischen Liturgik* (2 ed., 2 vols. Freiburg im Breisgau: Herder, 1912), I, 429.

CHAPTER II

LEGISLATION PRIOR TO GRATIAN

Upon leaving the previous discussion regarding the point of time at which there originated the use of the portable altar, one may next focus attention on the actual legislation enacted with reference to the portable altar. As was the case with very many other canonical institutes, so also with relation to the one which receives specific consideration here, its initial manifestations were of a purely local character. It was either some particular bishop, some diocesan synod, or some provincial council that utilized some occasion for the enactment of a law that sought either to establish a uniform rule, or to correct existing abuses which reflected a departure from the traditionally followed usage.

At the beginning of the preceding chapter mention was made of the first direct reference to the portable altar. That reference points also to the first legislation on the subject. The ordinance was indeed not a piece of legislation in the strict sense, but from a more inclusive viewpoint it may nevertheless be considered as a norm of law, since it was a precept given by the three bishops, Licinius, Eustachius and Melanius, with a view to regulating the actions of the missionaries in Brittany. These missionaries were ordered to cease using portable altars for Mass in the homes of the Bretons. Thus the first known ordinance regarding portable altars was an order which interdicted their use.[1]

For the proper evaluation of the text in question it must be pointed out that the particular abuse against which the bishops primarily inveighed was the practice which led women, in a manner similar to that of a deacon's service, to participate in the celebration of Mass. Thus the question of the use of the portable

[1] Amort, *Elementa Juris Canonici Veteris et Moderni, I,* 353–4. The letter reads in part as follows: " Relatione cognovimus, quod quasdam tabulas . . . circumferre et missas celebrare ibidem . . . praesumatis. . . . Repentina emendatio, sublatis dictis tabulis quas non dubitamus a Presbyteris consecratas, subsequatur."

altar, although it was definitely adverted to, constituted simply an incidental problem. For that reason no warranted conclusion may be drawn regarding any absolute prohibition against the use of a portable altar.

In the order of chronology the next text to be considered did not indeed imply any legislation, but its source and its content make it well worth mentioning here. It is taken from the works of Venerable Bede, who relates that in 692 two English missionaries among the Saxons on the continent carried with them sacred vessels and a consecrated slab of stone to serve as an altar.[2]

In Germany the first recorded legislation dates from the year 742. This legislation was enacted by a council held under St. Boniface (673–754). It ordered that only chaplains were permitted to accompany the army, and no other priests were permitted to go among the enemy except those who had been chosen for the purpose of saying Mass and fulfilling other sacred functions.[3] In the following year (743) the Council of Lestines (Estinnes, Lessines) in the County of Hainaut enacted the same ordinance.[4]

The appointment of chaplains for the kings, the princes, and their armies, was apparently a practice which was rooted in the tradition which had been established by the Emperor Constantine himself. In the present connection it should be stated that from the time of Charlemagne (742–814) direct mention was made of portable altars. In the camp of Charlemagne there was one: "Solemnis ara tum lignea tabula erat, quae linteo adaperto modum altaris effecerat."[5] Gattico reported that Robert II, King of the Franks (996–1031), had a portable altar of gold and silver, and

[2] Beda Venerabilis, *Historia Ecclesiastica,* lib. V, cap. 10: "Et cotidie sacrificium Deo victimae salutaris offerebant, habentes secum vascula sacra et tabulam altaris vice dedicatam."—*Venerabilis Bedae Opera Quae Supersunt Omnia* (ed. J. A. Giles, 12 vols., Londini, 1843–1844), III, 194. Cf. Thalhofer-Eisenhofer, *op. cit.,* I, 429; Braun, *op. cit.,* I, 73, 74.

[3] Mansi, *Sacrorum Conciliorum Nova et Amplissima Collectio* (53 vols. in 60, Parisiis, 1901–1927), XII, 366.

[4] Can. 1—Mansi, XII, 370.

[5] Mabillon, *Acta Sanctorum Ordinis Sancti Benedicti* (6 vols. in 9, Venetiis, 1733), II (*Miracula S. Dionysii,* saeculo III, cap. 20), 317. The text is quoted also by Braun (*Der christliche Altar,* I, 74) and referred to by Thalhofer-Eisenhofer (*Handbuch der katholischen Liturgik,* I, 429).

that Louis IX (1226–1270) had one at the gates of Jerusalem when that city was held by the Saracens.[6]

An indirect restriction, of doubtful authenticity however, hailed from England in the year 748, when Ecgbert, Archbishop of York (735–766), prescribed that no priest should say Mass in a private home or in any place other than a dedicated church.[7] But it is from a Capitulary of Charlemagne that a really definitive enactment derives. This Capitulary, which was held in the year 769, enacted that no priest was to presume to say Mass except in places dedicated to God, unless he was on a journey, and then he had to use a stone table consecrated by the bishop.[8] Gattico listed other capitularies of this same period,[9] the gist of which was that Mass should be celebrated only in places that had been dedicated to God by the bishop. In time of war an exception could be made. But even then, whenever possible, Mass was to be celebrated on altars consecrated by the bishop.

In the year 813 the Council of Chalon-sur-Saône, and in the year 816 the Council of Aix-la-Chapelle,[10] expressly reiterated canon 58 of the Council of Laodicea (343–381),[11] which ordered that Mass ought not to be said in private homes. This prohibition had been enacted with a view to curbing some existing abuses. As has been seen, the sickroom was often the scene for Mass in the early Church.

In order to gain a better understanding of the ninth-century legislation, it proves helpful here to take note of an observation made by Bliley. He stated that the permission to use the portable altar carried with it the permission to celebrate Mass in an unconsecrated place, whereas the prohibition to use a portable altar entailed simply the prohibition to celebrate Mass elsewhere than in a consecrated place. The factor around which the permission

[6] *De Oratoriis Domesticis et de Usu Altaris Portatilis,* cap. V, n. 8.

[7] *Excerpta,* n. 9.—Mansi, XII, 414.

[8] Can. 14—*Monumenta Germaniae Historica,* Legum Sectio II, *Capitularia Regum Francorum,* I (ed. A. Boretius, Hannoverae, 1883), p. 46 (hereafter cited *MGH*).

[9] *Op. cit.,* cap. V, n. 7.

[10] Can. 48—*MGH,* Legum Sectio III, *Concilia,* Tom. II, pars I (ed. A. Werminghoff, Hannoverae, 1906), p. 283; can. 84—*ibid.,* p. 368.

[11] Mansi, II, 582.

or prohibition turned was the consideration of celebrating Mass outside of a consecrated place.[12] He cited as an example of just such a piece of legislation the law of the VI Council of Paris, which was held in 829.[13] The celebration of Mass in houses or gardens was forbidden, except in the case of a journey when there was no church in the neighborhood, and when otherwise people would have been deprived of Holy Communion. But even then use was to be made of altars that had been blessed by the bishop.

In the same century, about 858, Herardus, Bishop of Tours, forbade the celebration of Mass in the home.[14] And shortly thereafter Hincmar, Archbishop of Rheims (845–882), forbade the offering of Mass in unconsecrated churches or in chapels not suitable for consecration, except in a case of necessity, and even then an altar of stone consecrated by the bishop had to be used.[15] Earlier in Basle, about 822, the statutes of Bishop Haito (802–823) permitted the celebration of Mass in private homes solely for the consolation of the sick.[16]

The first recorded hint that the use of the portable altar was beginning to get out of hand is found in the eighth canon of the Council of Metz in 888.[17] In that Council the celebrating of Mass in unconsecrated places of whatever nature was absolutely forbidden. The sickroom was mentioned explicitly, and concerning the celebration of Mass there it was stated "*quod omnimodis interdictum est.*" Relative to this point Martène added an interesting note. He stated that by way of substitution a *Missa Sicca* was offered in the sickroom.[18]

However, as proof that the drastic legislation of the Council of Metz was not universally regarded as necessary, one may point to

---

[12] *Altars According to the Code,* pp. 45–46.

[13] Cap. 47—*MGH,* Legum Sectio III, *Concilia,* Tom. II, pars II (ed. A. Werminghoff, Hannoverae, 1908), p. 641.

[14] Capitularium, cap. 34.—Mansi, XV, 503.

[15] Capitulare III, cap. 3.—Mansi, XV, 491.

[16] *Ahytonis Episcopi Basiliensis Capitulare,* can. 14.—*MGH,* Legum Sectio II, *Capitula Regum Francorum,* I, 364.

[17] Mansi, XVIIIA, 80.

[18] *De Antiquis Ecclesiae Ritibus,* lib. I, cap. III, art. 1, n. 16. Cf. also Gattico, cap. VI, n. 8.

a Council of Mainz, held in the very same year, which permitted the use of the portable altar not only in the sickroom but also in the open air, or also in a tent, when one was on a journey and no church was presently available. This was then a step toward leniency rather than strictness.[19] The importance of this legislation when enacted at Mainz was greatly overshadowed by the place of prominence that was later accorded to it at the hands of Gratian (+ ca. 1157).

[19] Mansi, XVIIIA, 67. The full text is: "In itinere vero positis, si ecclesia defuerit, sub divo, seu in tentoriis, si tabula altaris consecrata, ceteraque ministeria sacra ad id officium pertinentia adsunt, Missarum sollemnia celebrari permittimus."

CHAPTER III

LEGISLATION FROM GRATIAN TO THE COUNCIL OF TRENT

As just noted, the text from the Council of Mainz with its leniency regarding the use of the portable altar was to acquire a force which was to extend its application far beyond the confines of the province of Mainz. It was this text that was chosen by Gratian as being representative of the general law and practice of the Church on this point at his time.[1] It should be noted here that Gratian attributed the canon to the Council of Tribur (895). His error may have arisen through his borrowing of this text from the earlier collection of Burchard of Worms (+ 1025) or Yves of Chartres (+ 1117), both of whom had likewise listed the Council of Tribur as the source for this canon.[2]

C. 30, D. I., *de cons.*, furnishes the sole text to be found in Gratian's *Decretum* as dealing with the subject here under discussion. The importance of the text is thereby further increased, for in and by itself it reflects an accurate picture of the legislation then current. The *Decree* of Gratian, though as a collection it was never officially promulgated as the universal law of the Church, nevertheless enjoyed a much greater importance than would a present-day private collection. Its importance *de facto* was almost as great as if it had been promulgated officially. It was used in all the schools and chanceries as the last authority of appeal.

Since the earlier legislation on the portable altar was not uniform, and in relation to the various localities even contradictory, the acceptance of Gratian's text did amount to achieving the effect of a general legislation. The law as contained in this text was

[1] C. 30, D. I., *de cons.—Corpus Iuris Canonici* (ed. Lipsien. 2., post Aemilii Ludovici Richteri curas instruxit Aemilios Frieberg, 2 vols., Lipsiae: Ex Officina Bernhardi Tauchnitz, 1879–1881. Editio anastatice repetita, Lipsiae: Tauchnitz, 1922).

[2] Burchardus, *Decretum*, III, 56—*MPL*, CXL, 668; Ivo, *Decretum*, III, 59—*MPL*, CLXI, 210.

indeed enacted at a time when there was much concern in some quarters over the danger of abuse, of irreverence and of disregard for authority that seemed to be arising through the increased use of the portable altar. But evidently in the years that ensued up to the time of Gratian this threat never grew into the reality of an abuse, and thus this law's leniency became the accepted rule.

Subsequent centuries tell a different tale, for in the period between Gratian and the Council of Trent the use of the portable altar, both by the grant of the law and also through the benefit of custom, became so greatly augmented among the various religious Orders, as well as among the bishops and other dignitaries, that with this rapid expansion there arose many an abuse. The Council of Trent felt constrained to revise the current discipline with a single stroke of legislative authority, and to restrict the many liberties whose exercise formed the accepted usage.

At the time of Gratian the general attitude was rather that of extending than that of restricting the use of the portable altar. The far-reaching impact of this attitude is illustrated by the marked tendency in subsequent centuries to extend the privilege in many directions. Gratian had furnished the keynote of leniency, and it was this spirit that was to shape the general rule and usage until the time of the Council of Trent.

Before the time of Gratian the use of the portable altar was warranted, to a great extent, solely on the score of necessity. The same practice still obtained in Gratian's day. But with the changing times Christianity became more firmly established and less of a missionary enterprise in Europe, and thus a new situation of a different character was created. This had much to do with the fact that relative to the use of the portable altar there was introduced a new feature which took on the aspect of a privilege. The use of the portable altar was granted as a favor to certain high dignitaries, and also to others as a reward for services rendered to the Church. This added feature, the presence of which became noticeable even before the end of the twelfth century, has long since become the most prominent of the characteristics touching on the use of the portable altar. Today the granted right to the use of the portable altar has come to be designated simply as the privilege of the portable altar.

In this pre-Tridentine development a twofold division is readily suggested with reference to the privilege as granted to religious Orders and as granted to bishops. The former has a slightly earlier origin, so it will be treated first.

Pope Honorius III (1216–1227) on May 7, 1221, became the first Pontiff on record to treat of the portable altar when he granted to the Dominicans the privilege of using a portable altar as often as the need arose.[3]

Three years later this same Pope extended a similar privilege to the Friars Minor, so that they too might use portable altars wherever they happened to be.[4]

This extension of privileges did not take place without opposition. Many bishops viewed it as an infringement on their local jurisdiction, and demanded that their permission be secured before the privilege could be used. This practically had the effect of making the privilege inoperative. When the matter reached the attention of Pope Honorius, he wrote to the Bishop of Paris to clear up the point. This letter has been preserved for us in the Decretal Collection of Pope Gregory IX (1227–1241). Besides adding his own personal authority to the text, Pope Gregory enlarged it to include also the Dominicans, since the letter of Pope Honorius had mentioned only the Friars Minor.[5]

As phrased in the Decretal Collection, the privilege permitted the Dominicans and the Friars Minor to say Mass on a portable altar wherever they might be, and the Pope emphasized the fact that the privilege was not subject to any restrictive interpretation. Not a word was mentioned about the requisite existence of this or that necessity. The grant was made in the nature of a privilege pure and simple.

---

[3] Honorius III, const. *Postulastis a nobis*, 6 maii 1211.—*Bullarium Ordinis Praedicatorum* (opera T. Ripoll et A. Bremond, 8 vols., Romae, 1729-1740) I, 14, n. 24; Potthast (*Regesta Pontificum Romanorum inde ab Anno post Christum Natum 1198 ad Annum 1304* (2 vols., Berlini, 1874–1875), n. 6654 (hereafter cited Potthast).

[4] Honorius III, const. *Quia populares tumultus*, 3 dec. 1224—*Bullarium Franciscanum* (ed. I. H. Sbaralea, 4 vols., Romae, 1759–1768), I, 20; Potthast, n. 7325.

[5] C. 30, X, *de privilegiis et excessibus privilegiatorum*, V, 33.

Pope Sixtus IV (1471–1484) was the next to treat the question. He granted a further extension of the privilege to both Orders. He reiterated the general terms that Mass could be said in any decent place. He added that the privilege could also be used during the time of an interdict. The privilege was likewise extended to all members of the Second and Third Orders in so far as they could enjoy it.[6]

In 1265 the Carmelites obtained from Clement IV (1265–1268) the use of the portable altar in their oratories.[7] This privilege was extended by Urban V (1362–1370) in 1370 to permit them to say Mass in any decent place, provided that the Mass was celebrated in the presence of a bishop or some high civil authorities.[8] Next Sixtus IV enlarged the privilege so that they could use the portable altar at their own discretion in any suitable place for the benefit of either men or women.[9] Finally Clement VII (1523–1534) granted to all the members of the Carmelite Order of either sex the privilege of the portable altar, so that they could say Mass themselves or have it said by someone else in any decent place, even if the locality was placed under interdict.[10]

Other religious Orders enjoyed similar privileges. The Order of Canons Regular of the Lateran received the use of the portable altar for journeys or during the time of interdict.[11] The Carthusians received it from Pope Urban V, and the Jesuits from Paul III (1534–1549).[12]

---

[6] Sixtus IV, const. *Regimini efficaces,* 1474, n. 2—*Bullarum Diplomatum et Privilegiorum Sanctorum Romanorum Pontificum Taurinensis Editio* (24 vols. et Index, Augustae Taurinorum, 1857–1872) V, 224 (hereafter cited *Bull. Rom.*); Sixtus IV, const. *Regimini universalis,* 31 aug. 1474, n. 4—*Bull. Rom.,* V, 218.

[7] Clemens IV, const. *Urbi Dei,* 6 iun. 1265—*Bull. Rom.,* III, 732.

[8] Urbanus V, const. *In caritatis,* 8 iul. 1370—*Bull. Rom.,* IV, 528.

[9] Sixtus IV, const. *Dum attenta,* 28 nov. 1476—*Bull. Rom.,* V, 245.

[10] Clemens VII, const. *Ex clementi Sedis Apostolicae,* 12 aug. 1530—*Bull. Rom.,* VI, 147.

[11] Sixtus IV, const. *Dum ad universos,* 23 aug. 1476, n. 14—*Bull. Rom.,* V, 238; Iulius II, const. *Inter caeteras,* 2 apr. 1512, n. 26—*Bull. Rom.,* V, 522.

[12] Urbanus V, const. *Sincerae,* 25 apr. 1363—*Bull. Rom.,* IV, 520; Paulus III, const. *Licet debitum,* 18 oct. 1549—*Bull. Rom.,* VI, 396.

This enumeration may prove sufficient for illustrating how widespread the use of the privilege had become before the Council of Trent changed the whole matter. It may also be noted here that if any Orders had not received this privilege by direct concession, then they nonetheless enjoyed the possession of this privilege by way of participation with the others in what had been directly granted.

On the side of the commentators in their treatment of this privilege there is little that remains to be said. The point was eminently clear in the papal decretal issued by Pope Gregory IX, and thus the glossators sensed no profound need of any further explanation. Hostiensis (+ 1271) [13] in his treatment of this decretal dealt rather with the general laws about privileges than about this one in particular. He pointed out quite simply that a privilege must ever be interpreted in such a manner that it implies the grant of something. He likewise maintained that the Pope is above all bishops in his jurisdiction, and that accordingly they cannot by their authority restrict any of his grants.

Prior to the Council of Trent, then, the priest members of religious Orders were able to make free use of a portable altar in any suitable place. It is hardly to be wondered that abuses crept in. The privilege applied generally to all members of the institute and to all its branches. In the case of women regulars or also of men regulars who were not priests, the privilege implied that they could commission any priest to say Mass in their presence on a portable altar, even though he did not have the privilege personally. The privilege could be used by them even in interdicted localities, provided only that the religious community of which they were members had not furnished the cause for the interdict.

There remains now, as noted previously, the question of the use of the portable altar by bishops. It will be recalled that in the period prior to Gratian the bishop's chief part was in regulating the use of the portable altar. In fact, the very first direct reference to the use of the portable altar contained an order of several bishops to a pair of missionaries to desist from the use of the

---

[13] *Commentaria in Quinque Decretalium Libros* (5 vols., Venetiis, 1581), Vol. V, sub cap. 30, *de privilegiis*.

portable altar.[14] Most of the other pertinent texts were of the nature of espiscopal or conciliar legislation. A further check could be exercised by bishops through their control of the consecration of the altar as required at their hands.

Now all of this has been mentioned simply by way of preface to the acknowledged fact that what the bishops could permit others to do they could also do themselves. If they legislated on the use of the portable altar by their priests—and they certainly did, as has been shown—then that proved a sufficient warrant for them to use such altars themselves within at least the same limits. The legislators inherently possessed the power which they conferred on their subjects. It is impossible to state absolutely that they rationalized the point in just that manner, but the record of their actions seems substantially to indicate that. A fuller treatment of the point may be gleaned from the treatise written by Gattico.[15]

But after the appearance of the papal privilege as conferred on the Dominicans and the Franciscans, the same thing was granted to the bishops. It will be recalled that after Pope Honorius had granted the privilege of the portable altar to the Mendicants, he found it necessary to remonstrate with the local bishops for rendering the privilege nugatory by demanding that the religious secure the local bishop's consent before using the papal privilege. On the assumption that the bishops could withhold their consent even if there existed a papal privilege, the papal privilege would have proved valueless. Honorius insisted that his indult did not require the consent of the local ordinary to become operative.

It seems very likely that the circumstances which called forth this rebuke were the same that prompted Pope Boniface VIII (1294–1303) to grant the papal privilege of the portable altar to all bishops.[16] For if local ordinaries attempted to restrict the Friars in their use of this privilege, it is not unlikely that they might have raised the same obstacles for visiting bishops. In fact it seems from the text of the *Liber Sextus* that just such a situation was in effect, for the decretal contemplated precisely such bishops

---

[14] Amort, *Elementa Juris Canonici Veteris et Moderni,* I, 353.

[15] *De Oratoriis Domesticis et de Usu Altaris Portatilis,* cap. VII, nn. 1, 2. Cf. also Martène, lib. I, cap. III, art. 5, n. 7.

[16] C. 12, *de privilegiis,* V. 7, in VI°.

as were absent from their churches and dioceses, as though that were the reason for the privilege and the time when it was needed most.

Whatever the background happened to be, the privilege of the portable altar was granted in very liberal terms to all bishops by Pope Boniface VIII:

> Since bishops and their superiors frequently must absent themselves from their churches and dioceses for various reasons, and are not always conveniently able to get to a church to say or hear Mass, without which, unless reasonably impeded they ought never to pass a single day, we grant to them in this Constitution the privilege of having a portable altar, on which they themselves may celebrate and have others celebrate wherever they may be; and it is permitted to them to say or to hear Mass without falling prey to any violation of the local interdict where it obtains.

Noteworthy in this grant is the inclusion of the granted use of the altar by someone else as well as by the bishop. It seems that the privilege was applicable only while the bishop was on a journey, since that was the indicated reason for the papal grant. Moreover, the altar of which the bishop was granted the use was rather significantly designated as an "*altare viaticum.*"

In his gloss on this canon Ioannes Andreae (1272–1348) noted that the bishop was not to be absent from his diocese except for reasons of official business, since his traveling outside the diocese for any other reason was not warranted. He treated also of the similar privileges enjoyed by the Mendicants. Neither traveling bishops nor the Mendicants needed any permission from the local ordinary to use their portable altars. In an interdicted locality Mass was not to be said "*alta voce,*" nor were the interdicted people to be permitted to attend. Finally, the one who enjoyed the privilege of a portable altar could, if it proved expedient, say Mass at an earlier hour than was otherwise permissible.[17]

Panormitanus (1386–1453) likewise offered some comments in

---

[17] Glossa ad c. 12, *de privilegiis,* V, 7, in VI°—*Liber Sextus Decretalium D. Bonifacii Papae VIII suae integritati una cum Clementinis et Extravagantibus earumque Glossis restitutis* (Romae, 1582).

regard to this text. It was not enough to possess the consecrated stone itself; it was necessary also to have permission to use it. The bishop was empowered to grant the use of the portable altar to his priests. There was need also of the bishop's permission if the use of the portable altar proved in any way prejudicial to the rights of the churches which were under the bishop's jurisdiction.[18]

The words "*eorumque superiores*" in the text of Boniface VIII became the occasion for much commentary. They obviously referred to archbishops and patriarchs, but did they also refer to cardinals? That the latter were to be regarded as "*superiores*" is clearly seen from the fact that the term was generally thus understood. This is the position taken by Hynes in his reference to the doctrine presented by Gattico and Bliley.[19]

The reason why the text was generally thus interpreted may be set forth briefly. If the text had *not* meant to include cardinals under the word "*superiores,*" then there should have been some other text that did mention them, since cardinals had been using the portable altar for some time;[20] but no other text can be found among the papal documents of that period, all of which have been well preserved. The obvious conclusion is that there never was such a document. The word "*superiores*" in the text was accordingly meant to include cardinals, for just as they certainly do now, so they also did then, qualify for that title.[21]

Gattico[22] indicated the reason why the Pope should single out the bishops without mentioning their superiors by name. His theory was based on the circumstances that surrounded the grant. The grant was needed especially by the bishops inasmuch as it was they who more readily might be hindered from exercising

---

[18] *Commentaria in Quinque Libros Decretalium* (Venetiis, 1588), ad c. 30. X, *de privilegiis et excessibus privilegiatorum,* V, 33.

[19] Hynes, *The Privileges of Cardinals,* The Catholic University of America Canon Law Studies, n. 217 (Washington, D. C.: The Catholic University of America Press, 1945), p. 70; Gattico, cap. VII, nn. 6, 7; Bliley, *Altars According to the Code,* p. 48.

[20] Petra, *Commentaria ad Constitutiones Apostolicas* (5 vols. in 2, Venetiis, 1729), II, 276.

[21] Cf. Fagnanus, *Commentaria in Quinque Libros Decretalium* (Venetiis, 1696), ad c. 25. X, *de privilegiis et excessibus privilegiatorum,* V, 33.

[22] *De Oratoriis Domesticis et de Usu Altaris Portatilis,* cap. VIII, n. 8.

their rights when they were in the territory of another bishop. Residential bishops had been demanding that traveling bishops obtain permission for the use of the portable altar. Perhaps their equal rank lent impetus to this argument; in all likelihood they would not have dared interfere with the traveling cardinals, who were usually on papal business. In view of these circumstances Gattico felt that the Pope chose to direct the privilege to the bishops specifically.

Besides the grant of Boniface VIII, two other grants were made before the Council of Trent. They were issued for the benefit of papal dignitaries, the one being directed to the Auditors of the Rota, and the other to the Apostolic Referendaries.[23]

Thus the general discipline and practice prior to the Council of Trent was the following: In a case of necessity Mass could be celebrated almost anywhere on a portable altar. St. Thomas (1225–1274),[24] when commenting on Gratian's text, stated that Mass could be said outside of the church. St. Raymond of Pennafort (1175–1275) established a designated order of preference. If possible, then a consecrated church was to be chosen as the place for the celebration of Mass; if that was not possible, then a consecrated altar, or at least a "*parva tabula consecrata.*"[25]

That was the interpretation of the law with reference to the consideration of necessity. From the viewpoint of privilege, most of the religious orders had received it in very general terms, so that their priest members could say Mass in any decent place, similarly as the cardinals and bishops could do. These latter, moreover, could grant the same right to their inferiors. As the cardinals, the bishops and the theologians assembled for the Council of Trent, almost everyone enjoyed the right to use a portable altar. The abuses which in the meantime had developed were matter which awaited correction from the Council. With one stroke of legislation it indeed did accomplish a complete change in the discipline which had obtained until then.

[23] Gattico, *op. cit.,* cap. VII, n. 9.

[24] *Summa Theologica* (ed. Marietti, 6 vols., Taurini Romae: Marietti, 1937), III, q. 83, art. 3 ad 2.

[25] *Summa* (Veronae, 1744), lib. III, tit. XXIV, n. 6.

PART TWO:

LEGISLATION FROM THE COUNCIL OF TRENT TO THE CODE OF CANON LAW

CHAPTER IV

THE BISHOP'S POWER TO GRANT THE USE OF A PORTABLE ALTAR

While preparations for the Council of Trent were under way, it was suggested by a group of the Bishops of Italy that the Council should enact legislation that would prohibit the offering of Mass in private homes.[1] These bishops were not alone in feeling the need for such legislation. Pope Benedict XIV noted that Pope Paul III (1534–1549) had already given the matter consideration, and had appointed a committee of three cardinals and five other prelates to study the question.[2]

This committee after due consideration voted to refer the matter to the Council of Trent. It was there taken up in the Twenty-second Session with the result that a law was enacted which prohibited bishops from permitting Mass to be offered in private homes, or in any place, except in churches or in oratories dedicated solely to the service of God.[3]

Almost all of the authors who treat of this question agree that by this law of the Council of Trent the power of granting the use of a private oratory and, *a fortiori,* the power of granting the use of a portable altar was indeed taken away from the bishops.[4] The law itself was clearly stated, and it was later reaffirmed many times.[5]

---

[1] *Monumentorum ad Historiam Concilii Tridentini Collectio* (6 vols., Lovanii, 1785), V, *De Cultu Dei,* n. 7.

[2] *De Sacrificio Missae,* lib. III, cap. V, n. 10.

[3] Conc. Trident., sess. XXII, *de observandis et evitandis in celebratione missae,* cap. unic.: "Neve [Episcopi] patiantur privatis in domibus, atque omnino extra ecclesiam et ad divinum tantum cultum dedicata oratoria ab eisdem ordinariis designanda et visitanda, sanctum hoc sacrificium a saecularibus aut regularibus quibuscumque peragi."

[4] S. C. C., *Caesaraugustana et Matriten.,* 23 mart. 1907—*Fontes,* n. 4336; Benedictus XIV, *De Sacrificio Missae,* lib. III, cap. VI, n. 1; Fagnanus, ad c. 30, X, *de privilegiis et excessibus privilegiatorum,* V, 33..

[5] An authentic declaration of the Cardinal Interpreters of the Council of Trent, made in the year 1615 at the behest of Pope Paul V, stated that per-

The Council enacted no specific penalties for the violation of this decree. It merely decreed that the bishops were to proceed against all violators, whether they were secular priests or members of a religious institute.

Since the history of this legislation indicates that it was directed toward the restoration of reverence for the Blessed Sacrament and toward the edification of the faithful, it appears that the bishops retained the power to grant this privilege in a case of necessity, for that surely was a circumstance which lay beyond the scope and intent of the law in its restrictive character. That this was indeed the fact is clear from the responses of the various Sacred Congregations down through the years. For example, the Sacred Congregation for the Propagation of the Faith issued a directive against the abuses in Smyrna. In this directive it ordered that Holy Mass was not to be offered in private homes except in time of pestilence. In this latter circumstance there was simply needed the approval of the local Vicar Apostolic before the priest could proceed to the celebration of Mass in private homes.[6] A few years later, in 1765, the same Congregation decreed that both the regular and the secular clergy needed the bishop's permission in order to offer the Sacrifice of the Mass in private homes. Obviously there was implicitly acknowledged to the bishop the power to grant the needed permission.[7] In the year 1912 the Sacred Congregation of the Sacraments stated that an ordinary could permit holy Mass to be said in a private home, but not in a bedroom, and in 1915 the same Congregation added that this permission could be given for any day *per modum actus,* i.e., by way of concession for use on an individual occasion.[8]

---

mission for the saying of Mass in private oratories could come only from the Pope. The Council of Trent had withdrawn from all others the power of granting such a permission.—S. C. C., *Florentina,* 23 maii 1615—*Fontes,* n. 2396. Cf. also *Fontes,* nn. 280, 283, 413, 4336.

[6] S. C. de Prop. Fide, decr., 30 apr. 1753—*Fontes,* n. 4517; *Collectanea S. Congregationis de Propaganda Fide* (2 vols., Romae, 1907), n. 388 (hereafter cited *Collectanea*).

[7] S. C. de Prop. Fide (C. G.—Constantinop.), 18 nov. 1765—*Fontes,* n. 4547; *Collectanea,* n. 461.

[8] S. C. de Sacramentis, *Romana et aliarum,* 23 dec. 1912—*Fontes,* n. 2107; *Meliten.,* 22 mart. 1915—*Fontes,* n. 2110.

From these texts and other similar ones it is clear that the legislation of the Council of Trent, while it severely restricted the bishop's power to grant the use of the portable altar, did not abrogate it entirely. This was the view of the generality of the commentators.[9] If one contrasts the prohibition of the Council of Trent with these later decrees, it seems that the power of the bishop to make permissible the use of a portable altar became limited to the case of necessity. As Gattico indicated, the less suitable the place, the graver had to be the excusing cause. In his day even the Pope was not accustomed to permit the use of a portable altar for offering Mass in a bedroom.[10]

The necessity that was in question was not the extreme case of absolute urgency which of its very nature proved sufficient for the abrogation of human law, but rather the case which simply involved a great utility for a large group of the faithful. It was within the border zone that lay between a non-yielding law, on the one hand, and the necessity that knows no law, on the other hand, that the bishop's permission was required according to most of the authorities.[11] The reasons which they generally advanced in establishing the need of the bishop's permission were the considerations of a due surveillance with a view to the maintenance of a uniform practice.

If the bishop could not be reached, the vicar general was acknowledged as having the necessary power to grant the use of the portable altar in a case of necessity.[12] If neither the bishop nor the vicar general was accessible, then, according to the doctrine of Reiffenstuel (1642–1703), epicheia could be employed for the gaining of a practical decision in the case.[13]

---

[9] Cf. Ferraris, *Bibliotheca canonica, iuridica, moralis, theologica, necnon ascetica, polemica, rubricistica, historica* (Romae, 1885–1899), s. v. *altare;* Gattico, cap. IX, n. 3; Benedictus XIV, *De Sacrificio Missae,* lib. III, cap. VI, n. 1.

[10] Gattico, cap. IX, n. 3.

[11] Cf. Gattico, cap. IX, n. 8, who pointed to at least twenty-four authors who shared that view. Cf. also St. Thomas, *Summa Theologica,* Pars III, q. 83, art. 3, ad 2; Petra, *Commentaria ad Constitutiones Apostolicas,* II, 493.

[12] Petra, *loc. cit.,* n. 17.

[13] *Jus Canonicum Universum* (5 vols. in 7, Parisiis, 1864–1870), lib. III,

In order to prove that no permission was required in cases of extreme necessity, Gattico pointed to the manner in which one of the bishops of the Province of Calabria made his appeal to Pope Benedict XIV after an earthquake in 1743. Because so many churches had been destroyed by this disaster, the bishop petitioned the Pope to permit that the founded Masses which were to be said at ruined churches might be offered on portable altars until the churches could be rebuilt. The fact that the request did not relate to the use of the portable altar generally, although such a use was certainly necessary under the circumstances, indicated the bishop's realization of his possession of the requisite faculty to cover that need.[14]

The authors likewise discussed the reasons why and the circumstances under which the bishop could permit the saying of Mass outside of a church, and in consequence allow the use of a portable altar. To satisfy the needs of a great pilgrimage, to serve the faithful in a time of plague or of other calamities—these were reasons which they always listed. All the authors further agreed that an army encampment furnished a reason for the granting of the same permission by the bishop, but Cardinal De Lugo (1583–1660) contended that the bishop could grant permission for the use of a portable altar in an army camp solely on days of precept.[15]

The actual practice certainly abstracted from this restrictive view, probably because of the dangers both physical and moral that attended army life. It was accepted as a general rule that during a period of calamity it was the need of the people rather than the relative number of the destroyed churches that furnished the relevant factor in the shaping of an applicable norm, although quite usually the two factors coexisted, each of them pressing a rightful claim. The fact of a journey was not in itself a sufficient cause; in addition it had to involve the needs of a large group of people. Reiffenstuel explicitly stated that sickness did not serve

---

tit. 41, n. 13. Cf. Gattico, cap. IX, n. 11, who insisted that the rural dean or the pastor was to be consulted if no one else was available for the granting of the permission.

[14] Gattico, cap. X, n. 18.

[15] *Disputationes Scholasticae et Morales* (8 vols., Parisiis, 1868–1869), *De Eucharistia,* Disp. 20, sect. 2, n. 48.

as a sufficient cause, and that accordingly the ordinary could not grant permission for Mass to be said in a sickroom, for the law did not make it permissible even for him to say Mass in such a place.[16]

Generally a stronger reason was necessary for granting the use of a portable altar in a Christian country where churches were usually available than for granting it in a pagan country where the churches were few in number. And, finally, in grants which permitted the use of a portable altar in pagan lands it was not customary to restrict the use of the privilege to certain major feasts, as was done with reference to the granted privilege of a private oratory.[17]

---

[16] *Jus Canonicum Universum,* lib. III, tit. 41, n. 14.

[17] Cf. Gattico, cap. X, nn. 2 sqq.

CHAPTER V

THE BISHOPS' AND OTHER DIGNITARIES' PRIVILEGE TO USE A PORTABLE ALTAR

If, as has been seen, the Council of Trent limited very much the bishops' power to permit others to use a portable altar, did it also reduce or abrogate the personal privilege of using a portable altar, which privilege the bishops had received from Pope Boniface VIII? This question was raised soon after the closing of that Council, but the answer did not long remain in doubt, when in the year 1586 the Cardinal Interpreters of the Council were asked if the Council of Trent had abrogated the privilege of the portable altar as granted to bishops by Pope Boniface VIII. Further, it was asked if this same privilege could be used, not only when the bishops were outside their own dioceses, but also when the bishops were incapacitated by sickness. These two questions substantially related to everything that pertained to the bishops' privilege of the portable altar. The cardinals replied that the Council of Trent had not abrogated the grant of Pope Boniface VIII. They stated moreover that for a legitimate cause the bishops could also use the portable altar in time of sickness or of some other inconvenience.[1]

This state of affairs, namely the bishops' possession of the privilege of the portable altar for use at their own discretion, continued unchanged until the beginning of the eighteenth century. It was then that the pendulum swung briefly but sharply in the opposite direction under the reforming hand of Pope Clement XI (1700–1721). For it was this Pope who abruptly ordered an end to the abuses of bishops and regulars who, in unjustified reliance on the privilege as expressed in the *Corpus Iuris,* were saying Mass in forbidden places.[2] The prohibition then enacted was so sweeping that neither bishops nor cardinals were permitted to say

[1] Gattico, cap. XII, n. 2. Along with this reply Gattico listed also other similar responses.

[2] Decr. *Nonnulli,* 15 dec. 1703—*Fontes,* n. 264.

Mass in the houses of the laity even for the consolation of the sick.[3] This severe prohibition had been occasioned by various current abuses, as the decree clearly stated.

But the blanket prohibition did not long endure. It was only twenty years later that Pope Innocent XIII (1721–1724) declared that the words of Pope Clement ought not to be understood as forbidding a bishop to say Mass in the home of a lay person during his sojourn there. If a bishop was legitimately absent from his episcopal residence, he could regard the place where he sojourned as offering him whatever right he possessed in this matter at his own episcopal residence, and therefore could erect a portable altar for his celebration of Mass.[4] At a later time it was declared that a bishop needed only a reasonable and legitimate cause for the use of a portable altar in a private home.[5]

Authors uniformly agreed that even outside his own diocese a bishop could use a portable altar if it served his convenience to do so, despite the fact that without much effort a church was accessible. The long-standing customary practice in this regard warranted that opinion. Inasmuch as no limitations were expressed, it seems that the bishop could say Mass also in a bedroom or in the open air. The restrictions on the saying of Mass at sea will be considered in a later chapter.

The sense of the words of Pope Boniface VIII in granting the privilege to bishops " to celebrate the holy sacrifice of the Mass themselves or to have others celebrate it "[6] seemed to point to the permissible celebration of but a single Mass each day, so that the Mass could be offered either by the bishop himself or by someone else in the presence of the bishop.[7]

[3] Cf. S. C. C., *Caesaraugustana et Matriten.*, 23 mart. 1907—*Fontes,* n. 4336; Ojetti, *Synopsis Rerum Moralium et Iuris Pontificii alphabetico ordine digesta* (3 ed., 4 vols., Romae, 1909–1914), s. v. *altare portatile* (hereafter cited *Synopsis*); Reiffenstuel, lib. III, tit. 41, n. 6.

[4] Innocentius XIII, const. *Apostolici ministerii,* 13 maii 1723, § 24—*Fontes,* n. 280.

[5] S. C. C., *Caesaraugustana et Matriten.*, 23 mart. 1907—*Fontes,* n. 4336.

[6] C. 12, *de privilegiis,* V, 7, in VI°.

[7] Gasparri, however, was of the opinion that the celebration of two Masses was permissible, so that the bishop could himself offer Mass and in addition allow a priest to say Mass in the bishop's presence.—*De Sanctissima Eucharistia,* n. 268.

Coronata indicated the reason why the bishop had to be present if someone else said Mass. The privilege was a personal one which was meant for the benefit of the bishop. The same ruling obtained with reference to the same privilege enjoyed by cardinals.[8] An additional concession linked with the privilege of the portable altar as enjoyed by the bishops was the fact that all who were present when a bishop celebrated mass on a portable altar could by means of such an attendance satisfy the precept of hearing Mass on Sundays and feast days.[9]

The scope of this privilege was apparently limited inasmuch as Pope Boniface VIII had simply made mention of bishops who were absent from their sees. That seemed to limit the use of the privilege to bishops who were local ordinaries, but the authors generally agreed that the grant was intended for retired and titular bishops as well. The decisions of various Roman Congregations substantiated that view.[10]

Administrators of dioceses who were not bishops did not enjoy the privilege, but bishops-elect possessed it once they had been named in the Consistory, for from that moment they were held to possess the episcopal dignity, regardless of the question of their consecration as bishops.

As has already been shown, cardinals were included in the grant of Pope Boniface VIII, and like the bishops they continued to enjoy the use of the portable altar after the Council of Trent. Their privilege was reaffirmed in the year 1623.[11]

Other grants to the lesser dignitaries, such as the Auditors of the Roman Rota, which had been made before the Council of Trent were not affected by the conciliar decree, for they were direct papal concessions which had nothing in common with the question of competence on the part of the bishops. More will be said about these and other papal grants in the succeeding chapter.

---

[8] Coronata, *De Locis et Temporibus Sacris* (Augustae Taurinorum [Italia], 1922), n. 124.

[9] S. C. C., *Nullius,* 22 sept. 1640—*Fontes,* n. 2621; S. R. C., *Dubia de episcopis titularibus,* 25 aug. 1818, ad 1—*Fontes,* n. 5835; S. R. C., *Urbis et Orbis,* 8 iun. 1896—*Fontes,* n. 6261.

[10] Petra, *Commentaria ad Constitutiones Apostolicas,* II, 29, and IV, 22; Gattico, cap. XII, n. 20; Gasparri, *De Sanctissima Eucharistia,* n. 269sqq; S. R. C., *Dubia de episcopis titularibus,* 25 aug. 1818—*Fontes,* n. 5835.

[11] S. C. C., 18 febr. 1623—*Fontes,* n. 2436.

CHAPTER VI

THE USE OF THE PORTABLE ALTAR AS GRANTED THROUGH PAPAL INDULTS

In addition to the grants made by the various popes to the bishops and other dignitaries and to the religious, other concessions were from time to time given to individuals or small groups. The mere enumeration of such grants is pointless, but some of the general rules concerning them can profitably be stated here.

Papal concessions to the infirm and to travellers, which concessions permitted them to use a portable altar, represent the most common type. In the grants made for the benefit of the infirm the customary restriction demanded that, if possible, the Mass be said in a private oratory, for Mass was not to be said in a bedroom except in a case of the gravest necessity, so that the permission to offer Mass in a bedroom was indeed granted only quite rarely.[1]

The travellers who obtained permission to offer Mass on a portable altar were usually the missionaries in pagan lands or the priests who resided in localities whose population was violently anti-Catholic. But even then the granted permission was accompanied with restrictions as to place and circumstance relative to the act of celebration.[2] A decree of the year 1753, which was directed by the Congregation for the Propagation of the Faith against abuses in Smyrna, expressed many of these restrictions: Mass could be offered in private homes only in the time of pestilence, and even then only upon the permission of the vicar apostolic, upon his previous approval relative to the suitable character of the place, and upon due certification that the house was not inhabited by Jews, by heretics or by schismatics. Mass was not

[1] Benedictus XIV, ep. encycl. *Inter omnigenas,* 2 febr. 1744, § 22—*Fontes,* n. 339.

[2] S. C. de Prop. Fide (C. P. pro Sin.), 13 aug. 1669 (C. G.—Constantinop.), 18 nov. 1765—*Fontes,* n. 4484; n. 4547; *Collectanea,* n. 184; n. 461.

to be offered in a private home solely for the consolation of a sick person, since such a practice was too susceptible to abuse.[3] An elaboration of the latter point in a later decree clarified the fact that Mass could permissibly be said in the home of a sick person only when otherwise he would be deprived of the spiritual solace of Holy Viaticum.[4]

Because of scandal to the faithful and because of the danger of irreverence, the homes of Jews, of Moslems, etc., were not to be the scene of the Holy Sacrifice of the Mass except in cases of gravest necessity.[5]

Usually Mass could be offered only once a day on the portable altar, and the privilege did not ordinarily allow for the fulfilling of the precept of hearing Mass on the part of those who were in attendance when the privilege was used.[6] If a church was available, Mass was to be said there rather than on the portable altar; and even when a papal privilege was possessed by a priest, his use of the portable altar in a given place was conditioned on the previous approval of that place by the local bishop. This regulation was binding under pain of excommunication.[7] This legislation, however, was simply the general prescription; it was not binding

---

[3] S. C. de Prop. Fide, decr. 30 apr. 1753, nn. 2, 3—*Fontes,* n. 4517.

[4] S. C. de Prop. Fide, instr. (ad Ep. Scodren.), 11 sept. 1779—*Fontes,* n. 4581; S. C. de Prop. Fide, 14 dec. 1668—*Fontes,* n. 4480. The text of the latter decree runs as follows: "Cum sacrosanctum Eucharistiae Sacramentum a christianis infirmis expetitur, quaeritur:

1. An missionariis, in praedictorum infirmorum domibus, sacrificium Missae celebrare liceat.

2. An hoc procedat etiam cum mortis periculum urget, sed Viaticum, saltem occulte, deferri potest.

3. An licitum saltem sit, quando neque publice neque occulte deferri potest.

R. Ad 1. Non licere.

Ad 2. Non licere.

Ad 3. Tali casu licere, vel in domo infirmi, vel saltem in viciniori domo, si locus decens sit, ne infirmus Viatico privetur."

[5] S. C. de Prop. Fide (C. P. pro Sin.—Sutchuen.), 6 sept. 1821; litt. (ad Vic. Ap. Bosniae), 16 iun. 1827—*Fontes,* n. 4726; n. 4735.

[6] Reiffenstuel, lib. III, tit. 41, n. 18.

[7] Gattico, cap. XV, n. 8.

law for the bishops, for these could at their own discretion say Mass on a portable altar even when a church was readily accessible.

The question whether shipboard constituted a suitable place for the saying of Mass gave rise to voluminous commentary. Obviously the point was one which with the passing years offered new approaches for discussion in view of the rapid strides of progress that accompanied the science of shipbuilding. For a proper understanding of the legislation and the commentary on the celebration of Mass on shipboard one must duly bear in mind the point of time at which the legislation was enacted and the commentary supplied. In the past it was debated whether a special permission was needed for the use of the portable altar in the saying of Mass at sea when the requisite conditions of due decency and assured safety were fulfilled.

Gattico formerly inclined to the liberal opinion, which contended that no special permission was necessary, so that the granted privilege of the use of a portable altar carried with it also the right to say Mass at sea.[8] Even the while he proposed this doctrine he was conscious of a widespread opposition to it. He was eventually moved to abandon his opinion in consequence of the fact that the Holy See was known to have taken positive steps in the granting of a special permission for offering Mass at sea. This positive permission stressed the usual requisite conditions for the use of the portable altar. He reasoned that if the Holy See demanded something in addition to its postulation of these conditions, then clearly the ordinary granted privilege of the portable altar did not include the permission for offering Mass at sea.

Pope Benedict XIV admitted that there had indeed been room for discussion on the point, but he showed that the practice of the Church in its granting of the added permission had definitely removed all basis for a further discussion of the point.[9] The Church's practice of requiring a special permission was clear from many decrees.[10]

Gattico taught that the Holy See much preferred that Mass

[8] Gattico, cap. XI, n. 6.

[9] Benedictus XIV, *De Sacrificio Missae,* lib. III, cap. VI, n. 2.

[10] Eg., S. C. de Prop. Fide, 20 ian. 1667—*Fontes,* n. 4475; S. R. C., *Vicen.,* 4 mart. 1901—*Fontes,* n. 6309.

should be offered on the seashore rather than actually on board ship.[11] If Mass was celebrated on board ship, then the presence of an assistant priest was always called for. His office was to assist at the altar in safeguarding the contents of the chalice. As proof that the granting of permission for the saying of Mass at sea was rare, Pope Benedict XIV pointed out the fact that he knew of only two such grants which belonged to the time prior to the Council of Trent.[12]

But as shipbuilding improved, so that greater safety and security resulted, the privilege of saying Mass at sea was granted more easily. In fact, in modern times many of the larger luxury liners have their own chapels, but even in the twentieth century the mind of the Holy See is still that a special permission must be obtained for the celebration of Mass on shipboard, and this permission must be sought from the Holy See.[13]

---

[11] Gattico, cap. XI, n. 14.

[12] Benedictus XIV, *De Sacrificio Missae,* lib. III, cap. VI, n. 10.

[13] S. R. C., *Vicen.,* 4 mart. 1901—*Fontes,* n. 6309.

CHAPTER VII

LEGISLATION OF THE COUNCIL OF TRENT ON THE USE OF THE PORTABLE ALTAR BY RELIGIOUS

The exempt religious no longer possessed any privilege or exemption which could serve to hinder or to impede the removal of an abuse. With these words Pope Benedict XIV pointed to the effect of the law of the Council of Trent, which suppressed the privilege of using a portable altar, which privilege the religious had formerly possessed.[1]

The Council of Trent had found it necessary to deal energetically with a vexing abuse then current, namely the irreverence to which the Blessed Sacrament was being subjected through an injudicious and ill-advised use of the privilege of the portable altar. As the Fathers of the Council of Trent assembled to discuss this problem, they found that either directly by papal grant, or indirectly by way of participating with others in the granted privilege, almost all priests religious had the privilege of the portable altar for use in any safe and decent place, and apart from any previous permission from the local ordinary.

From this background came forth the law that bishops should not permit the Holy Sacrifice to be offered by any priests whatsoever, whether secular or religious, in private homes or in any place outside of a church or an oratory dedicated exclusively to divine worship and designated or approved by the local ordinary. No appeals, privileges, exemptions or customs whatsoever were to be urged against the bishop in this regard.[2]

Although this text of the Council seems clear enough, yet it furnished occasion for a controversy that raged mightily until the

---

[1] Benedictus XIV, ep. encycl. *Magno cum,* 2 iun. 1751, § 29—*Fontes,* n. 413.

[2] Conc. Trident., sess. XXII, *de observandis et evitandis in celebratione Missae,* cap. unic.

Holy See felt constrained to intervene for the sake of a definite solution. As is easily understandable, authors who belonged to religious institutes, whose priest members up to that time had enjoyed the privilege of saying Mass on a portable altar, could find occasion for interpreting the words of the Council of Trent as not depriving them of that privilege. They argued that, since their privilege was established for them in the *Corpus Iuris,*[3] the general formula of the Council, "*non obstantibus privilegiis,*" was not sufficient to abolish it. The bishop's task, they said, was to prevent abuses. Accordingly he could prohibit a particular religious from saying Mass on a portable altar, but religious as a body still retained their privilege. This argument was not without foundation, and in the light of present-day standards it could certainly be regarded as at least extrinsically probable because of the number of its proponents.[4]

But, if the words of the Council of Trent did not propose to abolish the privileges of the religious, it seems that they could have had little force at all. Apart from the bishops themselves, the religious were the chief recipients of the privilege of the portable altar, and it was the very breadth of their privilege that was the chief occasion for abuse. The decree would have had little or no worth if it did not comprehend the religious within the scope of its desired reformation. This was the line of reasoning followed by the Sacred Congregation of the Council.[5]

Although the question was not settled immediately after the close of the Council, the mind of the Church became increasingly clear in the decisions handed down by its various Sacred Congregations. For example, on July 9, 1619, the Cardinal Interpreters of the Council of Trent ordered certain regulars who had been saying Mass on a portable altar in a private oratory to cease from that practice.[6] Much clearer and more all-inclusive was the reply

---

[3] C. 30, X, *de privilegiis et excessibus privilegiatorum,* V, 33.

[4] Cf. Barbosa, *Iuris Ecclesiastici Universi Libri Tres* (3 vols. in 2, Lugduni, 1660), Vol. II, lib. II, cap. 7, n. 30 (hereafter cited *Ius Ecclesiasticum Universum*) ; Gattico, cap. XIII, n. 2. The latter author enumerated twenty-five authors who defended this view.

[5] S. C. C., *Caesaraugustana et Matriten.,* 23 mart. 1907—*Fontes,* n. 4336.

[6] Gattico, cap. XIII, n. 3.

of the Sacred Congregation of the Council given on June 4, 1672, to the Archbishop of Toledo, to the effect that the Council of Trent had indeed deprived the regulars of their former privilege by which they enjoyed the use of the portable altar even without the permission of the local ordinary.[7]

But the abuse continued in Italy and Sicily, so that another response of the same Congregation had to be directed thither. This informed the Archbishop of Messina that the regulars had no right to erect a portable altar in the room of a sick person, even of a fellow religious, without the consent of the local ordinary, or at least of the pastor of the territory.[8] In the following year the Archbishop of Naples was told that the religious could not, without his consent, use the limited privilege of a private oratory as equivalent to the general privilege of a portable altar, i.e., they could not say Mass in the private oratory on the days which had been excluded in the indult that granted them the privilege of the private oratory.[9]

But all these decrees were private responses, replies made to ordinaries perplexed by problems in their own dioceses. And despite them all the abuse of the unjustified use of the portable altar continued until Pope Clement XI issued a decree on December 15, 1703, that clarified once and for all the meaning of the decree of the Council of Trent. Reviewing the whole picture, the Pope lamented the fact that some religious, under the pretext of privileges, presumed to do things that were forbidden them. He first spoke of correcting the abuses in the use of private oratories. Then passing to the question of the misuse of the portable altar, he first called attention to the decrees of the Congregation of the Council which have here been recounted. Then he spoke of the privileges granted to the regulars in the Decretal Letters of Pope Gregory IX, which permitted them to use a portable altar and celebrate thereon without permission from the local ordinary. These same privileges, he said, were revoked by the Council of Trent, and therefore the religious were prohibited from using

[7] S. C. C., *Toletana,* 4 iun. 1672—*Fontes,* n. 2829.

[8] S. C. C., *In Messanensi,* 20 sept. 1698—Gattico, cap. XIII, n. 5.

[9] S. C. C., *In Neapolitano,* 30 maii 1699—Gattico, cap. XIII, n. 5.

them. Moreover the local ordinaries, as delegates of the Holy See, were to proceed against all violators, even the exempt religious.[10] These words were indeed definitive and unmistakable, but they were not unexpected. As Gattico noted, many authors in approaching the question without prejudice had already arrived at this same conclusion.[11]

That it was understood among some of the religious institutes that the Council of Trent had abrogated their privilege of using a portable altar is clear, for example, from the petition submitted by the Jesuits in the year 1579 to Pope Gregory XIII (1572–1585) for the renewal of their privilege. In granting their request that Pope stated explicitly that their old privilege had been abrogated by the Council of Trent.[12]

This early and explicit text which came so soon after the Council of Trent was argued away by some other regulars on the score that the privilege granted by Pope Paul III to the Jesuits had not been incorporated into the *Corpus Iuris*. But Fagnanus (1598–1678) pointed out that the Council of Trent had abrogated many privileges contained in the *Corpus Iuris* without explicitly mentioning the fact of their being found there. Therefore the inclusion or the lack of inclusion in the *Corpus Iuris* did not in any way affect the status of a privilege.[13] The same point was emphasized by Pope Benedict XIV [14] and by others. This doctrine with its evident implications was finally summed up in a decree of the Congregation of the Council.[15]

The same statement regarding the abrogating force of the decree

---

[10] Clemens XI, decr. *Nonnulli,* 15 dec. 1703—*Fontes,* n. 264.

[11] *Op. cit.,* cap. XIII, n. 8. Cf. Reiffenstuel, lib. III, tit. 41, n. 5; Barbosa, *Ius Ecclesiasticum Universum,* Vol. II, lib. II, cap. 7, n. 30; Fagnanus, *Commentaria in Quinque Libros Decretalium,* ad c. 30, X, *de privilegiis et excessibus privilegiatorum,* V, 33.

[12] Decr. *Usum altaris,* 1 oct. 1579: "Usum altaris viatici a f. r. Paulo Papa III concessum et deinde a Tridentino universe sublatum, vobis eatenus restituimus."—*Bull. Rom.,* VIII, 298.

[13] Fagnanus, *op. cit.,* ad c. 30, X, *de privilegiis et excessibus privilegiatorum,* V, 33.

[14] Ep. encycl. *Magno cum,* 2 iun. 1751, § 29—*Fontes,* n. 413.

[15] S. C. C., *Caesaraugustana et Matriten.,* 23 mart. 1907—*Fontes,* n. 4336.

of the Council of Trent had been made in the grant of Pope Pius IV (1560–1565) to the Canons Regular of the Lateran.[16]

But despite all these arguments it was not until the decree of Pope Clement XI that the point ceased to provoke spirited argumentation. He ended all the controversy by stating explicitly that the Council of Trent had put an end to the privilege of using a portable altar, which privilege the religious had formerly enjoyed. Since that avenue was now closed to them, the religious had to look elsewhere for a source whence they could derive the privilege of the portable altar. As can be gathered from the mention already made of the grant given to the Jesuits after the Council of Trent, that new source was accessible by way of direct petition submitted to the Holy See.

The legislation of the Council of Trent by its rigid discipline in this matter brought an end to the free and easy use of the portable altar as previously enjoyed by the religious. And just as in former years the leniency of the text in the *Decree* of Gratian had been the rule, so now the strictness of the decree of the Council of Trent became the norm for the succeeding generations. New grants of the privilege of the portable altar were relatively few, and those that were made were normally of a very restricted nature.

The first grant, as it has already been mentioned, came only two years after the closing of the Council. On March 8, 1565, Pius IV granted to the Canons Regular of the Lateran the privilege of the portable altar, to be permissibly used by them in the event of sickness. Any member of that institute when confined to his room by illness could offer Mass "*in proprio cubiculo,*" or could have another say it for him there. This also applied, "*servatis servandis,*" to the women of the Order.[17] Gattico, himself a member of this Order, noted that some authors claimed that the grant was a personal one, and hence could be used by a member of the community outside of his religious house. But he himself thought that the use of the privilege was simply localized for the house, inasmuch as the text spoke of those who were sick in the monasteries and priories of the institute.[18]

---

[16] Decr., 8 mart. 1565—Gattico, cap. XIII, n. 14.

[17] Pius IV, decr., 8 mart. 1565—Gattico, cap. XIII, n. 14.

[18] Gattico, cap. XIII, n. 15.

A later response of the Congregation of the Council supported this contention. This response stated that a portable altar could not permissibly be erected by a regular in a private home for the benefit of a sick regular.[19] If this can be taken as the mind of the Holy See, then it appears that the grant to the Canons was of a local rather than a personal nature.

But in the year 1725 this privilege was all but nullified by a decree of Pope Benedict XIII, which ordered bishops to use penal action against those religious who said Mass in their cells, notwithstanding any indults or customs to the contrary.[20] Nothing thereafter remained of the privilege, said Gattico, except in the case wherein the privileged religious had a suite of rooms which provided a place for Mass apart from the bedroom. The offering of Mass in the study, for example, was still permitted under the privilege.[21]

Another grant, of which mention has also been made, was that of Pope Gregory XIII to the Society of Jesus in 1579. This privilege permitted the Jesuits the use of the portable altar in any safe and decent place, even in an army camp. There were two limitations: the privilege could be used by only those priests who labored actively in the missions, and in addition the permission of the superior was always necessary.[22] Suarez (1548–1617) noted that this was a personal privilege, and rather extensive too, since it was made available to all priests of the Society while active in the missions.[23]

Rounding out the grants of the privilege of the portable altar as given after the Council of Trent, the authors listed merely a few additional ones. The first of these was the grant of Pope Gregory XIII to the Dominicans of the Polish Province. They were permitted the use of the portable altar wherever no churches were

---

[19] S. C. C., *In Messanensi,* 20 sept. 1698—Gattico, cap. XIII, n. 5.

[20] Benedictus XIII, decr. *Concilii Romani,* 1725—Gattico, cap. XIII, n. 16.

[21] Gattico, cap. XIII, n. 16.

[22] Decr. *Usum altaris,* 1 oct. 1579—*Bull. Rom.,* VIII, 298. Cf. Gattico, cap. XIII, n. 18.

[23] *In III Partem Summae D. Thomae,* Disp. 81, sect. 3—*Opera Omnia* (26 vols. et Index, Pariis, 1856–1878), XXI, 797.

available.[24] Pope Clement VIII (1592–1605) gave the Discalced Carmelites of Italy the same privilege, and Urban VIII (1623–1644) made a similar concession to the members of the Order of the Holy Trinity for the Redemption of Captives, but it was to be used by them only on their African missions.[25] In 1699 the Lithuanian Province of the Congregation of the Missions was granted the privilege of the portable altar for use in places where no churches were available.[26] And, finally, Barbosa (1589–1649) claimed that the Dominicans and Franciscans received anew the privilege of the portable altar "*vivae vocis oraculo*" from Pope Pius V.[27]

---

[24] Gregorius XIII, 20 iun. 1580—*Bullarium Ordinis Praedicatorum*, VII, 192.

[25] Gasparri, *De Sanctissima Eucharistia*, n. 262.

[26] S. R. C., *Congr. Missionum Provinciae Lituaniae*, 5 aug. 1699—*Decreta authentica Congregationis Sacrorum Rituum* (6 vols., Romae: Ex Typographia Polyglotta, 1898–1927), n. 2032.

[27] *Ius Ecclesiasticum Universum*, Vol. II, lib. II, cap. 7, n. 31.

CHAPTER VIII

THE USE OF THE PORTABLE ALTAR AS OBTAINED THROUGH PARTICIPATION IN PRIVILEGES

When one has compared the number and the universality of the grants of the privilege of the portable altar before the Council of Trent with the rarity of similar grants after that Council, especially as conferred on the religious, there readily arises the question whether there was not some other channel for the reception of this favor besides that of direct concession by papal indult. To this query many authors found an eminently satisfactory answer in the institute of the reciprocal participation in privileges as it obtained among religious.[1]

In order to achieve the present purpose it will suffice to recall that many Popes in times past rewarded this or that religious community by allowing it to share in all the privileges of some other community or group of communities. This practice was so multiplied by succeeding pontiffs, that finally all the various institutes shared in one another's privileges.[2] Such a general statement must naturally admit of exceptions. Whether or not the privilege of the portable altar falls under the general rule of this reciprocal participation and thus came to be shared by all religious will be examined here.

Since the grant of Pope Gregory XIII to the Jesuits was the widest concession of the privilege of the portable altar as made in favor of religious after the Council of Trent, it will be most profitable to trace its history to see if other religious groups came to possess the same privilege by way of mutual participation in it with the Jesuits. The first document of interest in the study of

---

[1] Coronata, *De Locis et Temporibus Sacris*, p. 127.

[2] For a detailed account of this history and development the reader is recommended to consult Matulenas, *Communication, a Source of Privileges*, The Catholic University of America Canon Law Studies, n. 183 (Washington, D. C.: The Catholic University of America Press, 1943).

this question is a constitution of Pope Pius V, written in the year 1571, in which he stated that the Jesuits were thenceforth to be reckoned with the Mendicants, and thus were to enjoy, by an act of reciprocal participation, the privileges held by the other Mendicants and the members of the other religious Orders.[3] The grant of the privilege of the portable altar was made to the Jesuits by Pope Gregory XIII in the year 1579. So at that time, at least, the Mendicants obtained the use of the portable altar by way of sharing in it with the Jesuits.[4]

However, only three years later the same Pope Gregory declared that, while the Jesuits could share in the privileges of the Mendicants, the converse did not obtain, i.e., the privileges granted to the Jesuits were not to be shared in by the other Orders.[5]

The wording of this constitution was not unmistakably clear. Did its ruling apply exclusively to the future, or did it also imply a loss of the privileges which had been gained in the past by way of reciprocal participation? Since the ruling implied a limitation of the acquired rights of the Mendicants, it seems that it was to be interpreted strictly. Accordingly it would not have put an end to the continued possession of the privileges that were already enjoyed by the Mendicants in virtue of what they shared in along with the Jesuits, for that effect was not explicitly stated in the ruling. The parallel case in this matter as adverted to in the Code of Canon Law[6] has been interpreted in this sense by the Pontifical Commission for the Interpretation of the Code.[7]

With the effect of furnishing occasion for added confusion, a constitution of Pope Clement VIII, given in the year 1597, apparently revoked the earlier constitution of Pope Gregory XIII.[8] Instead of clarifying the matter, this document seemed rather to

---

[3] Pius V, const. *Romanus Pontifex,* 18 nov. 1571—*Bull. Rom.,* VII, 636.

[4] Coronata, *De Locis et Temporibus Sacris,* p. 127.

[5] Gregorius XIII, const. *Pium et utile,* 22 sept. 1582—*Bull. Rom.,* VIII, 397.

[6] Can. 613, § 1.

[7] Responsum P. C. I., 3 dec. 1937—*Acta Apostolicae Sedis, Commentarium Officiale* (Romae, 1909-), XXX (1938), 73 (hereafter cited *AAS*).

[8] Clemens VIII, const. *Ratio pastoralis,* 20 dec. 1597—*Bull. Rom.,* X, 386.

confuse it the more, inasmuch as it did not explicitly mention the previous constitution of Pope Gregory. Because of the uncertainty thus occasioned, some authorities held that the privileges which had been directly granted to the Jesuits still could not be shared in by others.[9] On the other hand, those who contended that there was again restored the potential sharing on the part of others in the privileges granted to the Jesuits claimed that the abrogating clause of the constitution of Pope Clement was forceful enough to revoke any and all previously enacted restrictions.[10] Gasparri and Coronata, for instance, subscribed to this opinion.[11]

The doubt that exists about the original scope of the decree of Pope Gregory XIII, coupled with the probable revocation of that decree by Pope Clement VIII, seems to render the opinion safe that the privilege of using a portable altar which the Jesuits had obtained by direct concession was thereupon shared in by the other religious institutes, so that they all continued to enjoy it up until the Code of Canon Law. It is true that in the year 1732 Pope Clement XII (1730–1740) did revoke many privileges of the religious, but nowhere in this list of revocations did he make mention of the privilege of the portable altar.[12]

Matulenas traced the rapid growth and expansion of the interparticipation of privileges among religious until the benefits of this canonical institute extended to the congregation as well as to the Orders among religious.[13] He thereupon derived proof from an apostolic letter of Pope Pius XI (1922–1939) regarding the

---

[9] Reiffenstuel, lib. V, tit. 33, n. 33.

[10] Ferraris, s. v. *privilegium,* art. I, n. 27; Suarez, *De Legibus,* lib. VIII, c. XVII, n. 1—*Opera Omnia,* VI, 292; Matulenas, *op. cit.*, p. 112. The latter presents the argument at considerable length.

[11] Gasparri, *De Sanctissima Eucharistia,* n. 262, and footnote; Coronata, *op. cit.,* p. 127sqq. Cf. also Ojetti, *Synopsis,* s. v. *altare portatile,* n. 33; Barbosa, *Ius Ecclesiasticum Universum,* Vol. II, lib. II, cap. 7, n. 31sqq; Vermeersch-Creusen, *Epitome Iuris Canonici* (3 vols., Mechliniae-Romae: H. Dessain, 1937–1946), I, n. 713. These authors point to additional authorities.

[12] Clemens XII, const. *Romanus Pontifex,* 12 febr. 1732—*Bull. Rom.,* XXIII, 324; const. *Romanum Pontificem,* 29 mart. 1732—*Bull. Rom.,* XXIII, 325.

[13] *Op. cit.,* pp. 121 ff.

fact of the interparticipation of privileges before the Code of Canon Law; that Pontiff in confirming the privileges of the Jesuits specifically mentioned also those which they had received by way of sharing in what had been directly granted to other religious.[14]

Thus it seems to be fairly well established that almost all religious enjoyed the use of the portable altar within the limits of the original grant made to the Jesuits, namely, when the priest religious were actively engaged in mission work. It does not appear that any wider grants were made to avail for them since the time of the Council of Trent.

There remains to be considered a further implication relative to the question of privileges when they were held by being acquired through a sharing of them from others. The point may be of interest to secular priests inasmuch as they are eligible for membership in the various Third Orders Secular.

Certainly in the past at least those members of a Third Order who lived together in common life enjoyed a full participation in the privileges held by the First Order with which they were affiliated.[15]

Matulenas attempted to demonstrate that the same benefit of participation was later extended to include those members of the Third Order who lived at their own homes.[16]

He argued that when the V General Council of the Lateran (1512–1517) expressly limited the enjoyment of some of the participated privileges to those tertiaries who lived together in common life, the Council implied that apart from such an express limitation all tertiaries enjoyed the same privileges alike. The reasoning is faultless, but it seems to be without a solid basis in the text of the Council. The Council did not draw any comparison between the two groups of Third Order members, but rather spoke positively of the privileges of both of them. The wording of the Council did not lend itself to the drawing of any inferences about

---

[14] Pius XI, litt. ap. *Paterna caritas,* 12 mart. 1933—*AAS,* XXV (1933), 245.

[15] Sixtus IV, const. *Sacri Praedicatorum,* 26 iul. 1479—*Bull. Rom.,* V, 280.

[16] *Op. cit.,* p. 105.

a general rule on the question of privileges of the members of a Third Order.[17]

That point became one of purely historical interest however when Pope Leo XIII (1878–1903) reorganized the whole system of the Third Orders Secular. He revoked all their former privileges. Among the new ones he granted to them there was no mention of the privilege of the portable altar. So it seems certain that the members of the Third Orders Secular no longer possess it.[18] It is true that Pope Pius X (1903–1914) did once again permit the Third Order Secular of the Franciscans to share in certain privileges which were possessed by the First Order, but he did not include the privilege of the portable altar among the privileges regarding which he made favorable mention.[19]

The necessary conclusion seems to be that, although by way of participating in one another's granted concessions the religious Orders and congregations shared the privilege of the portable altar, the members of the Third Orders Secular were definitely barred, for lack of sharing and participating in the concessions made to the First Orders, from possessing the same privilege, namely, the use of the portable altar.

---

[17] Leo X, const. *Dum intra mentis arcana,* 19 dec. 1516 (Session XI of the Council)—Hardouin, *Acta Conciliorum et Epistolae Decretales ac Constitutiones Summorum Pontificum* (12 vols., Parisiis, 1714–1715) IX, 1834.

[18] Leo XIII, const. *Misericors Dei Filius,* 30 maii 1886—*Fontes,* n. 588.

[19] Pius X, decr. 8 iun. 1916—*AAS,* VIII (1916), 263; Coronata, *Institutiones Iuris Canonici* (2. ed., 5 vols., Taurini: Marietti, 1939–1947), I, n. 691c.

PART THREE:

THE LAW OF THE CODE ON THE USE OF THE PORTABLE ALTAR

CHAPTER IX

INTRODUCTORY OBSERVATIONS

As was noted in the introduction to the historical conspectus of this work, the liturgical aspects of the portable altar have already been treated at length in a Canon Law Dissertation.[1] These matters are therefore here taken for granted, and attention is directed rather to the canonical phases of the use of the portable altar.

It may be noted here, too, that the Code of Canon Law deals rather with the privilege than with the use of the portable altar. In the pre-Code legislation this terminology was not clearly defined, as can be seen from the history outlined in the preceding chapters. However, since the Code states[2] that all who enjoy the use of a portable altar do so by virtue of a privilege granted to them either by law or by indult, it is clear that the words "use" and "privilege" are now interchangeable in this connection. The word "privilege" is adopted because of the added notion that it conveys.

---

1 Bliley, *Altars According to the Code of Canon Law*, pp. 97 ff.

2 Can. 822, § 2.

CHAPTER X

CANONICAL COMMENTARY ON CANON 822, § 3

Article One: The Portable Altar Is Distinct from the Domestic Oratory

Although the privilege of using a portable altar is not identical with that of having a domestic or private oratory, the two have much in common. And since this very similarity could easily result in confusion of the two privileges, it may well be profitable here to point out the chief differences between them. The privilege of a domestic oratory points to the right of possessing a particular place reserved for divine services, whereas the privilege of a portable altar does not mean the right to possess a portable altar, but rather it carries with it the faculty of celebrating Mass in any decent and suitable place on an altar stone, and this especially outside of a church or oratory destined for divine worship.

The aforementioned truly radical difference between the two privileges underlies other variant features, which may be stated as follows:

1. The privilege of the portable altar includes the faculty of celebrating Mass in any decent place, i.e., not only in an unconsecrated place or unblessed location, but even in a place not destined for divine worship. The privilege of a private oratory, on the other hand, postulates a place reserved exclusively for divine worship, and one that is kept free from all profane uses.[1]

2. As a consequence of the foregoing it is clear that the privilege of a private oratory can in no wise involve the saying of Mass in a bedroom.[2] The privilege of the portable altar, however, as

[1] Cans. 822, § 3; 1196. Cf. Bliley, *Altars According to the Code of Canon Law,* p. 111.

[2] Coronata, *De Locis et Temporibus Sacris,* p. 79. There the author notes that a hospital ward could be an exception to this rule if the patients therein would otherwise be deprived of hearing Mass and receiving Holy Communion.

ordinarily granted by the Holy See, does not contain any such limitation. It is only when the Code authorizes local ordinaries to grant the privilege "*per modum actus*" that it forbids the use of this grant for the offering of Mass in a bedroom.[3]

3. A third difference which, like the first two, is an advantage of the privilege of the portable altar over that of a domestic oratory, consists in the fact that the law of the Code demands visitation and approval by the ordinary as a prerequisite for the use of a domestic oratory.[4] No such demands are made on a person who enjoys the privilege of a portable altar.

4. Those who assist at Mass said in a domestic oratory do not ordinarily fulfill their obligation of hearing Mass. This is a general rule, but the indult granting the privilege of the domestic oratory should be examined in every case, for it may very well state that servants and house guests, for example, can fulfill their precept of hearing Mass by attending a Mass offered in the domestic oratory.[5] However it is the opinion of some authors that assistance at Mass said by a priest who uses his privilege of the portable altar suffices for satisfying the precept.[6]

From these differences the advantages of the privilege of the portable altar over that of the domestic oratory are more apparent. It must be borne in mind that the ordinary domestic oratory is here under discussion, for the privileged oratory of bishops and others includes features that enhance its value to such an extent that it overshadows the portable altar.

A few of these features are the following:

1. Several Masses may be said on a single day in the domestic oratory of a bishop, whereas only one Mass is permitted in an unprivileged oratory or in virtue of a privilege of a portable altar.

2. Mass may be said in a bishop's oratory during his absence, not however on his portable altar.

3. The privilege of the portable altar which a bishop enjoys ceases at his death, but that of his domestic oratory remains.

---

[3] Can. 822, § 4; Coronata, *op. cit.*, p. 124.

[4] Can. 1195, § 1; Gasparri, *Tractatus Canonicus de Sanctissima Eucharistia*, I, 272.

[5] Can. 1249.

[6] Coronata, *op. cit.*, p. 124; Bliley, *op. cit.*, p. 112.

4. Finally, a bishop may have several domestic oratories, but only one portable altar privilege.

However these features of the domestic oratory of a bishop are not ordinarily contained in the privilege of a private oratory which the Holy See is wont to grant. Therefore it can be stated in general that the privilege of the portable altar is the greater of the two.

While the differences between the two privileges are being discussed, it seems warranted to mention one important similarity, namely that but one Mass a day is ordinarily permitted to be offered in a private oratory or in virtue of a privilege of a portable altar.[7] The reason for this fact in the latter case is that the privilege of the portable altar is a strictly personal privilege, and hence is intended to benefit primarily only the person to whom it has been granted.[8]

But even in this point the privilege of the portable altar has the advantage in that it can be used on any day, even the most solemn feasts, unless the indult by which it was granted should specify otherwise. The Code itself, on the other hand, forbids the offering of Mass in a private oratory on all the more solemn feasts.[9]

These observations on the similarity between the privilege of the portable altar and that of the private oratory may give a clearer picture of both of them, and hence may serve as a material aid in the presentation of the topic of the present work.

Article Two: The Portable Altar Must Be Used in a Decent and Suitable Place

By its very nature the Holy Sacrifice of the Mass demands the fulfillment of certain conditions before the celebrant can feel free to begin his chief work as another Christ. Before a man would presume to step forward to begin this greatest of all acts of divine worship, he is naturally going to see to it that the setting for his act is as decent and suitable as he can possibly make it. It is no wonder, then, that this very prompting of man's natural piety

---

[7] Cans. 1195, § 1; 1194.

[8] Coronata, *De Locis et Temporibus Sacris*, p. 125.

[9] Can. 1195, § 1.

finds concrete expression in the directions which the Code of Canon Law gives for the use of the portable altar.[10]

A Mass said on a portable altar is just as truly wonderful as a Mass offered in the most elegant cathedral. There is no intrinsic difference between the two, and hence in the case of the portable altar there is no lessening of the obligation to make the setting as suitable as the circumstances will permit.

Inasmuch as the foregoing remarks will prove sufficient for an introduction, it seems more profitable now to treat the subject matter of this chapter directly. A specific study of the various locations possible for the saying of Mass on a portable altar should do more towards illustrating the meaning of the text of the law than any abstract discussion of the terms "*honestus*" and "*decens*," which the Code uses. Let it suffice to say here that the general requisites are these: the location must be clean and properly fitted with all necessary furnishings for Mass, and it must also be safe and respectable.[11]

When actual or possible situations are considered in the light of these requirements, it is clear that the offering of Mass in public halls and auditoriums can very easily be done in such a manner as to satisfy the stated prerequisites. However, it is expressly forbidden to say Mass in the churches of heretics or schismatics.[12]

Authors writing before the Code had taught that Mass could not be said in the open air or underground for the reason that such locations were both unsafe and unsuitable.[13] The Code however states that this privilege permits the saying of Mass everywhere. The phrase, "*ubique celebrandi,*" accordingly seems to mean, at the very least, that the open air and the underground are not

---

[10] Can. 822, § 3.

[11] Coronata, *op. cit.*, p. 123.

[12] Can. 823, § 1. Cf. Augustine, *A Commentary on the New Code of Canon Law* (2. ed., 8 vols., St. Louis, Mo.: B. Herder Book Co., 1918–1924), IV, 172. There the author stated that even theaters could be used in the case of extreme necessity, but that Masonic temples are scarcely to be regarded as respectable places for saying Mass.

[13] Gasparri, *Tractatus Canonicus de Sanctissima Eucharistia,* I, 272; Cappello, *Tractatus Canonico-Moralis de Sacramentis* (3 vols. in 6, Vol. I, 4. ed., Romae: Domus Editoralis Marietti, 1945), I, n. 718, p. 677; Augustine, *op. cit.,* IV, 172.

automatically excluded as unsuitable places for the celebration of Mass. As a matter of fact, elsewhere in the Code the Mass which is said "*sub dio*" is mentioned as one of the places in which the Sunday precept can be fulfilled.[14]

Apropos of the phrase "*sub dio*" a considerable discussion has arisen among the authors concerning its exact meaning in this present connection. Although its classical and obvious meaning is "in the open air," certain authors strive to show that its meaning in Canon Law is really much broader than that. They would have it mean any place that is not strictly private, or even any place where Mass is said by reason of the privilege of the portable altar.[15]

Beste, in the passage just cited, simply states that "*sub dio*" means "*ubivis.*" He offers no argumentation in support of his claim. Coronata, likewise in the passage just indicated, delves into the point at some length. He argues that canon 1249 mentions only one place where the precept of hearing Mass cannot be fulfilled, namely a domestic oratory. No direct mention, so he continues, is made of the portable altar. The legislator was certainly aware of its existence, and hence must have intended to include it under the expression "*sub dio.*" In other words, his implication of the phrase is that the precept of hearing Mass can be fulfilled in any place where Mass is said on a portable altar, except in a private oratory. But this conclusion, though it seems established with some probable degree of acceptance, appears hardly justified by the premises.

In the first place, as Guiniven points out,[16] canon 1249 at least potentially excludes places other than private oratories by the very fact that it uses the expression "*sub dio*"; in other words, Coronata seems guilty of a *petitio principii* in his line of argu-

[14] Can. 1249.

[15] Beste, *Introductio in Codicem* (3. ed., Collegeville, Minn.: St. John's Abbey Press, 1946), p. 620; Coronata, *De Locis et Temporibus Sacris,* p. 294; De Meester, *Juris Canonici et Juris Canonico-Civilis Compendium* (nova editio, 3 vols. in 4, Brugis: Desclée de Brouwer et Soc., 1921–1928), III, pars I, n. 1166.

[16] *The Precept of Hearing Mass,* The Catholic University of America Canon Law Studies, n. 158 (Washington, D. C.: The Catholic University of America Press, 1942), p. 116.

mentation when he postulates in his premise the wide meaning for "*sub dio*," which meaning is the very thing that needs to be established. One can say that private oratories constitute the only exception invoked in canon 1249 solely on the assumption that "*sub dio*" means "everywhere."

Moreover, Coronata's added argument in which he appeals to the opinion of the pre-Code authors, namely that the precept of hearing Mass could be fulfilled anywhere, does not seem applicable. Such an appeal is valid only when the Code has not changed the earlier law. To hold that view Coronata manifestly had to assume that "*sub dio*" still means the same as "*ubivis*," which is precisely the point at issue. On the other hand, canon 18 explicitly states that ecclesiastical laws are to be understood according to their text and context.[17] If the meaning of the words themselves is clear, then no interpretation is necessary. In view of the fact that the expression "*sub dio*" was not found in the previous legislation on this matter, the pre-Code authors naturally could not comment on it in the sense of an expression which in law was held to be the equivalent of "*ubivis*." [18]

It seems better, then, to take the expression "*sub dio*" in its obvious meaning, as referring to Mass said in the open air. That this is, in fact, actually the mind of the Holy See is evident from documents issued since the publication of the Code. The faculties granted to chaplains during the late war included that of saying Mass in a decent place, "*etiam sub dio et in navi.*" That "*sub dio*" means precisely "in the open air" is clear from the next clause of the faculty. That clause reads, "taking precaution, however, when Mass is said '*sub dio*,' to prevent the particles of the Most Blessed Sacrament from being blown away by the wind, using for that purpose a tent with flaps descending on three sides of the altar." [19]

The question involved in canon 1249, namely that which regards

---

[17] "Leges ecclesiasticae intelligendae sunt secundum propriam verborum significationem in textu et contextu consideratam . . . ."

[18] Guiniven, *op. cit.*, pp. 36 ff.

[19] S. C. Consist., *Index facultatum*, 8 dec. 1939, n. 2—*AAS*, XXXI (1939), 710. Cf. Bouscaren, *The Canon Law Digest* (2 vols., Milwaukee, Wis.: The Bruce Publishing Co., 1934–1943), II, 607.

the possible fulfillment of the Sunday precept in connection with the use of the portable altar, will be traced at length in a subsequent chapter. Let it suffice here to point out the established fact that under the present law the open air can rightfully be considered a suitable location for the offering of Holy Mass.

The same reasoning whereby it has been concluded that Mass may now be said in the open air is also valid for proof that subterranean rooms of one kind or another are not automatically excluded as places in which Mass may be offered. There is no longer any evident reason why in themselves the open air and the underground are not respectable and safe as locations for the saying of Mass.[20]

What is to be said regarding the celebrating of Holy Mass in a bedroom? It has already been seen that the Code in canon 822, § 3, states that the privilege of the portable altar may be used anywhere except at sea. Taking these words at their face value, some authors [21] have concluded that Mass may indeed be said on a portable altar in a bedroom. Their argument seemed to be strengthened by the text arrangement of the next paragraph of the canon, which speaks of the ordinary's faculty for granting the use of the portable altar under certain conditions and "per modum actus." In this grant to the ordinary the Code expressly excludes from his faculty the right to allow the saying of Mass in a bedroom. That there is no mention of such a restriction in the preceding paragraph would seem to force the conclusion that the general indult granted by the Holy See for the use of the portable altar does include the permission to offer Mass in a bedroom. However a recent Instruction of the Sacred Congregation of the Sacraments [22] has the effect of rendering the above opinion no longer tenable. In the Instruction the Sacred Congregation lists a number of exact conditions the presence of which the local

---

[20] Cappello, *De Sacramentis,* I, n. 718, p. 677.

[21] Bliley, *Altars According to the Code of Canon Law,* p. 111; Hynes, *The Privileges of Cardinals,* p. 72; Coronata, *De Locis et Temporibus Sacris,* p. 127.

[22] S. C. de Sacramentis, instr. *Quam plurimum,* 1 oct. 1949—*AAS,* XLI (1949), 493–511.

ordinary must verify before applying to the Holy See for the grant of the privilege of the portable altar to one of his subjects. The second of these conditions requires that a petition for the use of a portable altar for saying Mass in a private home shall not involve the offering of the Holy Sacrifice in a bedroom. The fourth condition involves the same requirement when the privilege is sought on behalf of an infirm priest.[23] It would be permissible, however, to say Mass in a room that would in ordinary parlance be designated as a bedroom when, as a matter of fact, the room is not ordinarily *used* for sleeping purposes, because the Instruction says: "semper tamen excluso cubiculo, in quo quis dormire solet."[24]

The next article of this chapter will be devoted entirely to the question of the use of the portable altar at sea. This separate treatment seems warranted in the light of the twin elements of practical importance and changing legislation on the topic.

On the matter of the saying of Mass on railroad trains, in airships or in airplanes, authors do not have much to say. Those who do mention the point, however, are well agreed that a modern train can certainly afford a decent and suitable place for the saying of Mass, and that the Sacred Species can be treated with all due reverence.[25] Those authors feel, however, that a train trip of some days' duration is necessary.

Just why this should be so is not evident. It seems that a priest when traveling all day Sunday could certainly use his privilege of the portable altar. It seems that he could also do so even if the duration of his railroad trip simply covered the full time on Sunday morning when Mass can permissibly be said. The permitted or forbidden use of the privilege depends on the presence or absence of the elements of decency and safety in the situation. A long journey would most certainly be a contributing factor in war-

---

[23] S. C. de Sacramentis, instr. *Quam plurimum,* 1 oct. 1949, II, 9, a, b—*AAS,* XLI (1949), 504, 505.

[24] S. C. de Sacramentis, instr. *Quam plurimum,* 1 oct. 1949, II, 9, a—*AAS,* XLI (1949), 504.

[25] Cappello, *De Sacramentis,* I, n. 712, p. 671; Coronata, *De Sacramentis,* I, 257. The latter recalls that as a chaplain in the I World War he often had occasion to say Mass on hospital trains.

ranting the use of the privilege, but of greater importance as such a factor would be the welcome opportunity for fulfilling the Sunday precept. The question of the length of the trip might very well enter into the discussion when the priest wishes to use the privilege of the portable altar on week days. Assuredly a trip of but one or two days' duration during the week would less readily justify a coping with the risks that admittedly attend the saying of Mass under such unusual circumstances.

Though airships no longer enjoy the vogue that once was theirs, it is still historically noteworthy that papal permission was granted to Father Paul Schulte, O.M.I., to celebrate Mass for the first time on an airship on May 8, 1936, during the transatlantic voyage of the dirigible *Hindenburg* from Friedrichshafen to New York.[26]

On the question of the offering of Holy Mass in airplanes there has appeared in the Catholic Press a news item from the Vatican City. It reads as follows:

> The Sacred Congregation of the Sacraments has declared that it has given absolutely no authorization for Masses aboard airplanes, the Vatican radio reports. The reasons given were that, because of the short time involved in flight, priests can easily celebrate Masses before or after a flight, and that frequent sudden motions of aircraft would hamper the celebrant. The Congregation pointed out that special permission is required under canon law for Masses in sea voyages (Canon 822).[27]

The Apostolic Delegate possesses no faculty by which he may permit a priest to offer Mass in an airplane. Moreover, it is clear from the quoted news release that the Holy See does not feel that an airplane is as yet a safe place for the celebration of Holy Mass. Both the reasons cited by the Sacred Congregation are by their very nature not permanent, and it may well be that the future will bring a relaxation of this present prohibition.

---

[26] Bouscaren, *The Canon Law Digest,* II, 203. Cf. *America,* 23 May, 1936.

[27] *The Denver Register* (Denver, Colo.), Nov. 28, 1948.

Article Three: The Privilege Does Not Include the Saying of Mass at Sea

The privilege of the portable altar permits the saying of Mass in any decent and suitable place except at sea.[28] This last phrase, "*non tamen in mari,*" points to the sole exception as found in the present general law, and it will be the subject of discussion in this article. It does not embody a new restriction or involve any new legislation; it is carried over from the pre-Code law, in which it reflects its very early origin.[29]

This limitation is obviously based on an understandable doubt in the mind of the legislator, namely whether or not due reverence for the Holy Sacrifice could be maintained while a ship was subject to the uncertain buffeting of the winds and the waves. As was noted earlier in Chapter Six, with the improvement of shipbuilding techniques the permission to offer Mass at sea was more readily granted, but the Holy See still demanded that such permission be obtained.[30] The mind of the Holy See continues to be the same on this question. At present however the faculty may be obtained from the Apostolic Delegate.[31]

It is to be noted that in the wording of this faculty no mention is made of the necessity of an assistant priest, nor is the priest's stateroom automatically excluded as being unsuitable.

Although the word "*mare*" was classically always understood to mean the sea or the ocean, authors have adduced various reasons in order to show that this word should not be taken in that strict sense in the present connection. That is to say, when canon 822, § 3, mentions the sea as being the only place in which the privilege of the portable altar cannot be used, it does not mean to imply that

---

[28] Can. 822, § 3.

[29] Gasparri, *Tractatus Canonicus de Sanctissima Eucharistia,* I, 272; Ojetti, *Synopsis Rerum Moralium,* 1, 337; cf. *supra,* pp. 36, 37.

[30] S. C. C., *Vicen.,* 4 mart. 1901—*Fontes,* n. 6309.

[31] *Faculties* (*Private*), c. IV, n. 37: "To permit priests who are journeying either by sea or over streams to celebrate Mass on board ship on a portable altar, provided there be nothing unbecoming about the place where the Mass is celebrated, and there be no danger of the spilling of the Precious Blood."—Bouscaren, *Canon Law Digest,* I, 182.

the privilege may be used while its possessor is voyaging on lakes or streams.

There are two reasons advanced by the authors in support of this contention: 1) the term "ocean voyage" has been interpreted in another connection as including also travels on lakes and rivers,[32] and 2) an even more cogent reason is found in the phrasing of the Indult by which the Apostolic Delegate grants the use of the portable altar at sea. It reads: To permit priests who are journeying either by sea or *over streams,* to celebrate Mass on board ship on a portable altar . . . ."[33]

Unless the added expression in the granted faculty be acknowledged as meaningless, this faculty applies equally to sea voyages properly so called and to voyages undertaken on lakes and rivers. If it does so apply, then the ordinary indult to use a portable altar is of no use to one who is traveling over any inland bodies of water. In other words, the phrase, "*non tamen in mari,*" of canon 822, § 3, must be understood broadly as excluding the use of the privilege of the portable altar on any body of water whatsoever.[34]

One final question concerning the celebrating of Mass at sea remains for discussion. The norm, in the past as well as in the present, by which men have always decided whether or not Mass could be said under a given set of circumstances has been the thought of the reverence due to the Blessed Sacrament. As times change and as scientific advancements of all kinds are made, certain situations which previously were considered to be unsuitable for Mass can now be regarded as suitable. This has already been demonstrated in the case of Mass said in the open air or underground, but it is nowhere more clearly seen than in the case of Mass at sea.

Mass was at first said on the shore with the ship anchored nearby. Then, as shipbuilding progressed, the saying of the Mass was transferred to the boat itself, an assistant priest being dutifully on guard against the possible spilling of the Precious Blood. Still

---

[32] S. C. de Prop. Fide, 27 iun. 1914 (*Sylloge,* n. 51)—Bouscaren, *Canon Law Digest,* II, 219.

[33] *Faculties* (*Private*), c. IV, n. 37—Bouscaren, *Canon Law Digest,* I, 182.

[34] Hynes, *The Privileges of Cardinals,* pp. 73 ff.

later the construction of ships reached such a state of development through the huge gyroscopes which serve to keep them on an even keel, that the presence of an assistant priest was no longer required. Ultimately permission was granted for the erection of permanent semi-public oratories [35] on board some of the larger ships, such as the *Rex* and the *Conte di Savoia.*

This last fact occasioned some interesting conclusions from the side of the authors who discussed it. The question that arose was briefly this: Did the existence of a semi-public oratory on board a ship obviate the necessity of a priest's obtaining an indult in order to say Mass aboard that ship in its oratory? An answer in the affirmative seems warranted for the reason that the prohibition of Mass at sea was framed within the law which related to the rightful use of the portable altar, and not within the law which touched the celebrating of Mass in a semi-public oratory.

In addition, the reason behind the law's prohibition was the danger of irreverence, which danger must have been judged non-existent by the authorities who granted permission not only for the erection of the semi-public oratory, but also for the reservation of the Blessed Sacrament therein. A law loses its binding force when the whole reason for the law ceases to exist. This is the line of argumentation adopted by Cappello in the most recent edition of his work,[36] and it represents a complete reversal of his previous position.[37] Coronata likewise discusses the question in his recent work *De Sacramentis,* and agrees that the reasoning and opinion of Cappello do not lack probability.[38] This, too, on the part of Coronata, represents a veering away from his earlier view.[39]

Both Cappello and Coronata, as cited above, go even a step farther. They argue that on a ship which has a semi-public oratory priests who possess the privilege of the portable altar may indeed use it to say Mass in their staterooms or elsewhere without

---

[35] Coronata, *De Sacramentis,* I, n. 224, p. 211.

[36] *De Sacramentis,* I, n. 712, p. 671.

[37] Cappello, *De Sacramentis,* I (3. ed., Romae: Marietti, 1938), n. 753.

[38] Coronata, *De Sacramentis,* I, n. 257, p. 228.

[39] Coronata, *De Locis et Temporibus Sacris,* p. 78. Cf. Hynes, *The Privileges of Cardinals,* p. 75.

having obtained a special indult to say Mass at sea. The same argument is again advanced: If the boat is safe enough to permit therein the erection of a semi-public oratory, then the whole reason for the canonical prohibition against the saying of Mass at sea has ceased, and accordingly the privilege of the portable altar can be used.

The one serious objection against this line of reasoning is that which is raised in the very words of canon 21, according to which such laws as are enacted in view of a general danger remain in force even if in a particular case the danger does not exist.[40] This objection is not directly met by the authors cited above. But in all probability they would reply that the point in question does not represent an isolated or a particular case, but rather a large portion of the whole field covered by the law. Accordingly the restrictive norm of canon 21 could well be regarded as not properly applicable.

Though no authors have availed themselves of this line of argument, its validity hardly seems challengeable with apodictic effect. The ultimate conclusion of this argument could be formulated thus: If a large ocean liner in fact connotes a suitable place for the erection of a semi-public oratory, then, whether or not an oratory has in fact been erected, a priest traveling on such a liner could use his privilege of the portable altar even apart from a special indult which allows the celebration of Mass at sea. If the ship is in every way suited as a place for the erection of a permanent chapel in which the Blessed Sacrament could be properly reserved, then the whole basis for the prohibition against the use of the portable altar has ceased, and accordingly the use of the privilege seems duly warranted. This is exactly the same reason which the authors adduce for the conclusion they reached in the kindred situation they treated, and thus there seems to be no reason why the same argument should be deemed inapplicable here.

It may be objected that besides the danger of irreverence involved in saying Mass at sea there is another reason underlying the prohibition, namely, that the Holy See desires to maintain an immediate vigilance over the situation. However, it seems that

---

[40] Cf. Hannan, "Holy Mass Aboard Ship," *The Jurist* (Washington, D. C., 1941-), VIII (1948), 70.

such a purpose could be alleged in all laws, at least in those which definitely restrict liberty. In this particular case such a purpose would seem to rest on the primary purpose, for it is because of the danger of irreverence that the Holy See wishes to maintain vigilance. If the danger is non-existent, in the judgment of the Holy See itself, then also the reason for the vigilance is no longer in evidence.

The contemplated situation is one in which the advancements in modern science have established facts for which the mind of the law has not yet explicitly accorded a general acceptance. To the writer it seems by no means improbable that these facts will gain increasing acceptance from the generality of commentators. Once that has happened, one may with a considerable degree of assurance assume that what is now implicit in the law will then be explicit as well, for the law as it stands in this matter relies upon what the common estimation is ready to accept as established fact. Until such time one will well-advisedly be slow to make a personal application of logical but untried theories.

CHAPTER XI

CANONICAL COMMENTARY ON CANON 822, § 4

Loci Ordinarius aut, si agatur de domo religionis exemptae, Superior maior, licentiam celebrandi extra ecclesiam et oratorium super petram sacram et decenti loco, numquam autem in cubiculo, concedere potest iusta tantum ac rationabili de causa, in aliquo extraordinario casu et per modum actus.

Article One: Granters of the Privilege

Proceeding in orderly fashion in its treatment of the privilege of the portable altar, the Code next comes to a discussion of the faculties of local ordinaries and of major superiors for granting the use of the portable altar.

A cursory perusal of the last paragraph of canon 822 will convince the reader that it represents an attempt of the legislator to make provision for unusual circumstances, which by reason of their diversity and unpredictability cannot be governed by the preceding general norm.

With this purpose in mind, the legislator logically puts the matter into the hands of the local ordinaries and major superiors. These men are presumed, and legitimately so, to be in closer contact with the general law in its application *de facto* under existing conditions. It is these men, too, who will, by virtue of this canon, have the means to cope with such situations in the way most beneficial to the souls involved.

Canon 198 contains a complete enumeration of all who are included under the term "local ordinary." It embraces residential bishops, abbots and prelates *nullius* and their vicars general, apostolic administrators, vicars and prefects apostolic as well as all those who function in the stead of any of the foregoing during an interregnum. All these men, then, by virtue of their office are empowered to grant the privilege of the portable altar under the limitations set forth in the fourth paragraph of canon 822.

The major religious superiors in exempt institutes who may grant the privilege of the portable altar are those who receive mention in canon 488, n. 8. They are the abbot primate, abbots who are superiors of monastic congregations, abbots of independent monasteries which pertain to some monastic congregation, the superior general of any religious institute, the provincial superiors and their vicars, and finally all others who have the same jurisdiction as does a provincial superior. All these come under the title of major superiors.[1] These superiors posses the same faculty for conferring the use of the portable altar on their subjects as do the local ordinaries for theirs. However, the use of the power which these superiors have is limited to the confines of a house of their own religious institute; they cannot authorize their subjects to use a portable altar for saying Mass in any place not owned or controlled by the institute in question. In such cases the competent authority for issuing the privilege is the ordinary of the place in which the religious wants to say Mass.

Since the faculty as conferred on the local ordinary by canon 822, § 4, implies the possession of an ordinary power,[2] there readily can arise an occasion on which the ordinary may see fit to delegate this power to a parish priest.[3] Such a delegation would certainly be in line with the previously noted purpose of canon 822, § 4, which is to provide for special contingencies beyond the scope of the general law. To this end the local ordinaries are supplied with the faculty to grant the use of the portable altar, and for the more perfect attainment of that end these same ordinaries are empowered to pass on this faculty to their priests if that method should prove advantageous to the common good.

If one studies this portion of legislation one must indeed be impressed with the thought and the work that has gone into it, and be reminded that, even while the Church acts in its legislative capacity, it is still mindful that its entire *raison d'être* is the salvation of souls.

---

[1] Bliley, *Altars According to the Code*, p. 116.

[2] Can. 197, § 1. Cf. Guiniven, *The Precept of Hearing Mass*, p. 131.

[3] S. C. de Sacr., resp., 29 iul. 1927, *adnotationes—AAS*, XX 1928), 80, 81.

Article Two: Restrictions of Place

Those things which have already been treated in the preceding chapter concerning the place for the use of a portable altar reflect the general law on the subject. They are the fundamental rules generally applicable in all situations, and accordingly must be applied here too. It is natural that all the limitations with reference to the place of celebration as applicable in connection with the general indult for the use of the portable altar should be carried over and applied to the permission which the bishop may grant under certain limited circumstances. Moreover, a further restriction is expressly placed on the bishop in that he cannot grant the use of the portable altar for the purpose of offering Mass in a bedroom.[4] This restriction is not new with the Code. It is found in a decree which the Sacred Congregation of the Sacraments issued in the year 1912.[5] But it had taken root long before then, for Gattico when writing almost two centuries earlier, had noted that in his day the Pope did not customarily permit the use of the portable altar for celebrating Mass in a bedroom.[6]

In the pre-Code legislation an exception to the prohibition against the celebrating of Mass in a bedroom was made when other means were not available whereby a sick person might receive holy Viaticum.[7] Assuredly under similar circumstances in the present day the same exception would still obtain.

The bishop's inability to permit Mass to be said in a bedroom does not imply any disability in the use of his own personal privilege in the matter. In granting the privilege of the portable altar to cardinals and to bishops the Code does not except from that privilege the faculty of celebrating Mass in a bedroom.[8] However, the recent Instruction of the Sacred Congregation of the Sacraments, *Quam plurimum,*[9] seems to set down as a general

---

[4] Can. 822, § 4.

[5] S. C. de Sacramentis, *Romana et aliarum,* 23 dec. 1912—*Fontes,* n. 2107. Cf. *supra,* p. 29.

[6] Gattico, cap. IX, n. 3.

[7] S. C. de Prop. Fide, 30 aprilis, 1753—*Coll.,* n. 388.

[8] Cans. 239, § 1, n. 7; 349, § 1, n. 1.

[9] Cf. *supra,* pp. 60 ff.

rule that a bedroom is not a fit place for the celebrating of the Holy Mass with all due reverence. Moreover this statement is made by the Sacred Congregation prior to any discussion of the various titles under which the privilege of the portable altar may be enjoyed.[10] It seems definitely then to apply as well to the privilege enjoyed by law as to that enjoyed by indult.

An additional restriction of the local ordinary's faculty of allowing the celebration of Mass outside a church or oratory was reflected in a reply of the Sacred Congregation of the Sacraments in 1926. The Congregation declared that the ordinary cannot by virtue of canon 822, § 4, permit the celebration of Mass in a home in the room in which a deceased person is laid out, except in some extraordinary case when a just and reasonable cause is present.[11] By way of explanation the Congregation further declared that the conditions of an extraordinary case and of a just and reasonable cause could obtain in the event of the death of a residential bishop, or of a member of the royal family, or of a person outstanding in merits through his benefactions to the Church or the State, or through his very liberal donations to the poor and the needy, or, lastly, on the occasion of the death of a person who had received from the Holy See the privilege of having Mass said in his private house. In all of these cases the ordinary could permit one or two Masses, or at the most three, to be offered in the room of the deceased. In every case the usual funeral service was to be held in the church.[12]

These remarks may serve as a sufficient answer for any questions that may arise on that phase of the local ordinary's faculty which relates to the factor of place when he grants the use of the portable altar outside of a church or an oratory. Whatever has been said about the local ordinary applies equally to the major superiors of exempt religious communities under the conditions in which these can grant a similar use of the portable altar.

---

[10] S. C. de Sacramentis, instr. *Quam plurimum,* 1 oct. 1949, II, 1—*AAS,* XLI (1949), 501.

[11] S. C. de Sacramentis, 3 maii 1926—*AAS,* XVIII (1926), 388.

[12] Cf. Coronata, *De Sacramentis,* I, n. 258, p. 230; Woywod, *A Practical Commentary on the Code of Canon Law* (10. printing, 2 vols., New York: Joseph F. Wagner, 1946), II, 621, (j).

Article Three: Other Restrictions Found in the Law

Before exploring the other restrictions which the Code places on the bishop's power to grant the use of the portable altar, the writer wishes to call attention to two things. The first of these is the fact that, since canon 822, § 4, contains an exception from the law as stated in canon 822, § 1, which prescribes that Mass must be said in a church or an oratory, it must be interpreted strictly. This is a clear application of canon 19, which has moreover been expressly corroborated by the Holy See.[13]

The second of these is the fact that, with reference to the type of cause which is requisite to warrant the ordinary's use of this faculty, the Code has not effected any alteration in the pre-Code legislation. Some authors had concluded that the earlier law was changed inasmuch as the present law requires only a just and reasonable cause for the granting of the permission, whereas the earlier law demanded a grave cause. Taking cognizance of the uncertainty existing among the authors on this point, the Sacred Congregation of the Sacraments clearly asserted that canon 822, § 4, confirms the traditional discipline of the Church with regard to the gravity of the cause which must be present before the ordinary can grant the use of the portable altar.[14]

In the annotations officially published by the same Sacred Congregation the question is discussed at some length, and the reasons underlying the response are clearly delineated. These annotations furnish the following statement:

> If one considers that not only the reason for the permission must be just and reasonable, but besides that the permission must be given only by way of act, and only in an extraordinary case, it can reasonably be inferred that there is no change in this respect. For the gravity of the cause, or necessity, is to be taken in moral estimation; and since c. 822, § 4, requires not only that the cause be just and reasonable, but that the permission be granted by the ordinary only by way of act and

---

[13] P. C. I., 16 oct. 1919, ad XII—*AAS,* XI (1919), 478; S. C. de Sacramentis, *Romana et aliarum,* 3 maii 1926—*AAS,* XVIII (1926), 389.

[14] S. C. de Sacramentis, litt. ad Rev.mos Ordinarios Italiae, 26 iul. 1924 —*AAS,* XVI (1924), 370–371.

> in some extraordinary case, surely we have then a case of moral necessity. And therefore no change has been introduced in the old law and jurisprudence.[15]

Such a clear statement from the Sacred Congregation definitely terminates all argument relative to the measure of gravity which the cause must offer if it is to make the granting of the permission sustainable in law. Moreover, it leaves no doubt that, at least as far as the requisite cause for the granting of permission is concerned, the opinion of the pre-Code authors is still to be followed.[16]

In this connection Guiniven points out [17] that, when the pre-Code authors considered what cause was required for the legitimate use of the faculty on the part of the bishop, they invariably stressed the factor of the postulated need of the faithful to fulfill the precept of hearing Mass. The examples they gave all seemed to assume the presence of a sufficient cause only when the church was destroyed, when it had become too small to accommodate all the faithful, when because of pestilence Mass could not be said in the church, etc.[18] In fact, Gasparri could not see how a sufficiently grave necessity could exist unless it involved necessarily the obligation of the faithful to fulfill the Sunday precept.[19]

Guiniven does not state his own views on this question. This is not at all strange, for he was exclusively concerned with the precept of hearing Mass. The foregoing argumentation clearly shows that the need for the fulfillment of this precept offers a sufficient cause on the side of the ordinary for the granting of permission to celebrate Mass outside of a church or an oratory.

---

15 S. C. de Sacramentis, *Romana et aliarum,* 3 maii 1926, *adnotationes,* ad I—*AAS,* XVIII (1926), 389–390. (Translation as contained in Bouscaren, *Canon Law Digest,* I, 388.)

16 Can. 6, 3o.

17 *The Precept of Hearing Mass,* p. 123.

18 St. Alphonsus, *Theologia Moralis* (ed. L. Gaudé, 4 vols., Romae, 1905–1912), lib. VI, n. 356; Many, *De Missa,* n. 6.

19 Gasparri, *De Sanctissima Eucharistia,* I, nn. 276, 278. Cf. Many, *De Missa,* n. 6, 2o, where he entertained the opposite view. Cf. also Van Hove, *Tractatus de Sanctissima Eucharistia* (2. ed. Mechliniae: Dessain, 1941), pp. 346, 347; Regatillo, *Ius Sacramentarium* (2 vols., Santander: Sal Terrae, 1945–1946), I, n. 220.

However the view of the Holy See as expressed by the Sacred Congregation of the Sacraments does not seem to coincide altogether with that of Gasparri. When this Congregation reviewed the discipline of the Church with regard to the place for the celebration of Holy Mass, it adverted in the following manner to the limited faculties conferred on the local ordinaries by canon 822, § 4:

> . . . the faculties of Ordinaries in this matter are rather limited, and may not be exercised except in an extraordinary case, nor without just and reasonable cause, which must be inspired by the highest motives connected with divine worship and the spiritual welfare of the faithful. . . . Hence, it is beyond doubt that there would not exist the just and reasonable cause which is required by c. 822, if the celebration of Mass outside a church were desired on the occasion of some profane celebration, or to add solemnity to some celebration of a purely political nature. In such circumstances the celebration of Mass outside a church is absolutely forbidden by c. 822. And this is even more true if the occasion in question has by its very nature any suggestion of superstition, or any feature which is dangerous to right religious sentiment or to the purity of the faith of Catholics. . . . In such cases the Ordinary of the place should inform the parties concerned that he has no authority to grant their request; and if they insist, urging special considerations of time, place, or person, he should refer their request to this Sacred Congregation of the Sacraments, which shall decide the matter.[20]

Although the letter of the Sacred Congregation does not explicitly draw any conclusions, yet the fact that it excludes only profane celebrations and those of a purely political nature from the category of the just and reasonable cause required by canon 822 seems to indicate that several possibilities still remain. The whole tenor of the letter points to this. Moreover, if the necessity

---

[20] S. C. de Sacramentis, litt. ad Rev.mos Ordinarios Italiae, 26 iul. 1924 —*AAS*, XVI (1924), 370, 371. (Translation as contained in Bouscaren, *Canon Law Digest*, I, 385–386.)

of fulfilling the precept of hearing Mass were the only just and reasonable cause for which the ordinary might act, then the language of the Code would indeed be needlessly obscure, and that of the Sacred Congregation would definitely be misleading.

From this line of reasoning the writer feels safe in concluding that besides the necessity of fulfilling the Sunday precept there are other causes which can rightly induce the local ordinary to employ his faculty of permitting the celebration of Mass outside of a church or an oratory. Such causes which evince an entirely religious nature, or whose profane character is at the same time accompanied with religious considerations, seem to meet the requirements. Certainly in the former category one would place a Field Mass celebrated on the occasion of a Holy Name Rally, or of a jubilee celebration for a beloved ordinary. Causes that seem to come safely within the latter class are the celebration of Mass in connection with a Catholic War Veterans' Convention or a Boy Scout encampment, and the celebration of Mass on some day of national, historical importance by way of an act of thanksgiving. Although in such cases the fulfilling of the precept of hearing Mass be not the motivating cause for the granted permission, it is nevertheless possible for those in attendance to meet their obligations in this matter on a Sunday or feast day of obligation. The question regarding the fulfillment of the precept of hearing Mass will be treated *ex professo* in Chapter Fourteen.

Taking the restrictive phrases of canon 822, § 4, in the order of their successive arrangement, one next comes upon the phrase "in an extraordinary case." Guiniven, in taking up his explanation of this point, found that authors had nowhere treated it in the light of conditions in America.[21] Even American authors who had treated this matter limited their discussion to examples which are so truly and universally extraordinary that there can be no doubt regarding their validity in furnishing a sufficient cause, though some doubt could perhaps be cast on their complete fitness in that respect.[22]

---

[21] *The Precept of Hearing Mass,* p. 128.

[22] Cf. Bouscaren, "De Missa ex licentia Ordinarii celebrata,"—*Periodica de Religiosis et Missionariis* (Brugis, 1905–1919); *Periodica de Re Canonica et Morali Utili praesertim Religiosis et Missionariis* (Brugis, 1920–1927);

The core of the difficulty lies in the fact that the word "extraordinary" is a relative term. A thing is extraordinary only in relation to some standard. The question, then, is whether the case must be an extraordinary one in relation simply to some particular diocese or territory, or whether it must be such in reference rather to the whole Christian world. The importance of the choice of standards that one sets is obvious.

Many situations that are more or less commonplace in this country are extraordinary if viewed in the perspective of the universal Church. By way of concrete example one may point to a parish which in a predominantly urban diocese has had a sudden influx of people occasioned by a large housing project within its territorial limits. The parish church is now totally inadequate. Can the ordinary permit the saying of extra Masses in an adjacent auditorium? The solution of the problem will depend on whether or not the situation can be classed as extraordinary.

Judged by the present-day standards, especially as they exist in the large eastern dioceses of this country, the situation occurs all too frequently to be considered extraordinary. Hence, if conditions as they exist within the diocese are to furnish the standard of what is ordinary and what is extraordinary, then it seems that in the example given the bishop does not have the power to permit the celebration of Mass outside of a church. The solution seems to be, however, that the standard of what is ordinary and what is not must be gauged in the light of conditions as they exist throughout the entire Church.[23]

This conclusion is based on the fact that the Code legislates for the universal Church, and that therefore the "extraordinary case" which it demands in canon 822, § 4, need simply be extraordinary in relation to the universal Church. As Guiniven argues,[24] if a bishop in an enactment of a diocesan synod gave a faculty that could be exercised only in an extraordinary case, then it would seem that the case would have to be judged in relationship to that diocese alone. Similarly, if a plenary council issued a similar

---

Periodica de Re Morali, Canonica, Liturgica (Brugis, 1927–1936; Romae, 1937–), XXVIII (1939), 58 (hereafter cited *Periodica*).

[23] Regatillo, *Ius Sacramentarium*, I, n. 220.

[24] *The Precept of Hearing Mass*, p. 128.

decree or faculty, the case most probably would have to be extraordinary in relation to the country in which the council was held. Finally, if the Code, the law of the universal Church, has such a faculty, the norm of what is ordinary and what is extraordinary should be measured in relation to the general conditions in the whole Church. Fortified, then, by this line of reasoning, one can say with regard to the example given above that, when the faculties of the parish church are overtaxed, the bishop has it within his power to permit Mass to be said outside of church at least temporarily.

The restriction which is implied for the ordinary's faculty in the phrase "*per modum actus*" as contained in canon 822, § 4, constitutes the subject matter for the ensuing paragraphs of this article.

The consideration of the intrinsic and extrinsic arguments that must be weighed if one is to determine the meaning of the phrase *per modum actus* leads one to the view that the theoretical and practical solutions of the difficulty do not necessarily coincide. The phrase *per modum actus* is traditionally opposed to that of *per modum habitus.*[25] Yet this fact does not shed adequate light on the precise meaning of *per modum actus,* since the phrase *per modum habitus* is also very difficult to interpret. Because of the lack of a clear definition of the phrase *per modum actus,* it will prove helpful to delimit its meaning in a negative fashion by ascertaining what things the phrase does not imply.

It is certain that the local ordinary cannot grant permission for Mass to be celebrated perpetually outside of a church or oratory. Likewise it is certain that he cannot by a single act permit Mass to be said outside of a church for any extended duration of time. There can be no doubt that such a permission would be granted *per modum habitus.* Moreover, it is improbable that the ordinary can grant permission for Mass to be said outside of a church *durante causa,* at least if the cause will endure for more than a few weeks.

So much is reasonably certain. Guiniven advances very strong arguments to support his view that the controversial phrase *per*

[25] Regatillo, *Ius Sacramentarium,* I, n. 220.

modum actus must be taken at face value, and hence must be interpreted to mean that the concession can be made for only one act, i.e., that the permission can be granted for but one celebration of Mass outside of a church or an oratory.[26]

His opinion is based on the fact that canon 822, § 4, must be interpreted strictly. The strict interpretation appears indeed to call for the close limitation which contemplates the celebration of a single Mass.[27] Corroborative proof is found in the annotations officially published in connection with a response of the Sacred Congregation of the Sacraments. There the consultor argued from the legislation of canon 1194, which grants the bishop power to allow only one Mass to be said in domestic oratories. If in oratories only one Mass could be permitted by the ordinary, while outside of oratories and hence outside of sacred places altogether the celebration of more than one Mass were permitted, there would seem to be a want of harmony in the law.[28] The weakness of that argument seems to consist in the fact that the permission to say Mass in a private oratory connotes a privilege which is intended for purely private interests, whereas most of the situations which involve the bishop's granting of the use of the portable altar concern the public interest.

Whatever cogency these arguments may have, it is nevertheless a fact, as Guiniven himself admits, that they are rarely employed by the authors.[29] The strict interpretation as offered by Guiniven has strong support in theory, yet in practice there seems tenable a more lenient interpretation which leaves the granted permission for the celebrating of Mass to be available for use at least several times.[30] Even the Congregation of the Sacraments implicitly countenanced this opinion, for in the above-cited response it stated

[26] *Op. cit.*, p. 130.

[27] Regatillo, *Ius Sacramentarium,* I, n. 220. This author upholds the opposite view, but he does not offer any arguments in support of it.

[28] S. C. de Sacramentis, resp. 3 maii 1926, *adnotationes—AAS,* XVIII (1936), 391.

[29] *The Precept of Hearing Mass,* p. 131.

[30] Lehmkuhl, *Theologia Moralis* (9. ed., 2 vols., Friburgi Brisgoviae: Herder, 1898), II, 167; Vermeersch-Creusen, *Epitome Iuris Canonici,* II, n. 552; Regatillo, *Ius Sacramentarium,* I, 220; Bastnagel, "Cases and Studies," *The Jurist,* II (1942), 157.

that on certain occasions the ordinary may permit one or two Masses in a funeral chamber, but never more than three.

By way of practical solutions for the situations that exist in this country it may be said that, if the emergency exists for only a short time, the ordinary can renew his permission every two or three weeks. A much more workable arrangement is based on the fact that this power given to the ordinary by canon 822, § 4, is an ordinary power, hence can be habitually delegated.[31] If it is foreseen that the emergency will continue, the ordinary can delegate to the local pastor the powers granted him by canon 822, § 4. The pastor can then repeatedly *per modum actus* provide for the needed celebration in a building which is not a semi-public oratory.[32] It is clearly the mind of the Holy See however that the ordinary apply to the Holy See for a special indult if the emergency manifests any tendencies toward a quasi-permanency.[33]

In similar situations in missionary countries the Holy See, through the ministry of the Sacred Congregation for the Propagation of the Faith, is accustomed to give to ordinaries a special faculty by which they can allow priests and missionaries to say Mass outside of churches and oratories. If the bishops of these territories could solve the difficulty simply by giving the permission *per modum actus* in virtue of canon 822, § 4, then the Apostolic Faculties would seem to be unnecessary.

When the Apostolic Faculties were granted in 1929 to the Ordinaries of Latin America, Pope Pius XI stated that the new faculties were drawn up with due relation to the law of the present Code. This list of faculties embodied one by means of which priests could be allowed the use of the portable altar for the benefit of the faithful wherever churches were lacking or remained at a great distance. In the light of the existing law of the Code this grant quite plainly implied that under the extant circumstances the already possessed faculty of allowing, *per modum actus,* the

---

[31] S. C. de Sacramentis, *Montis Regalis in Pedemonte,* 5 ian. 1928, *adnotationes—AAS,* XX (1928), 80.

[32] Cf. Bastnagel, "Cases and Studies," *The Jurist,* II (1942), 157.

[33] S. C. de Sacramentis, decr. *Romana et aliarum,* 3 maii 1926—*AAS,* XVIII (1926), 370.

celebration of Mass outside of churches was not deemed adequate for meeting the present emergency.[34]

All these arguments indicate in very strong fashion that, while the *per modum actus* application of the ordinary's faculty to grant the use of a portable altar need not be limited to single acts, yet when the situation has any aspect of permanency about it, this faculty should not be used. The bishop should rather apply to the Holy See for a special indult.

In this country several of the Western dioceses have, in fact, obtained various indults from the Holy See to provide for exigencies in their own territories. The priests of the Diocese of Fargo have enjoyed since 1927 the privilege of the portable altar, and this privilege is made available to them for use in any decent place except at sea. The priests of the Archdiocese of Omaha and of the Dioceses of Reno, Salt Lake, Crookston and Winona have the faculty, with various limitations, of saying Mass in the rectory during the winter months because of the hardships attendant on the celebrating of Mass in the churches during that season. Priests of the Diocese of Winona may say Mass on a portable altar in impassable places and also in institutions under civil jurisdiction.[35]

These faculties have been granted in order that the needs of each particular territory may be duly and adequately consulted. The grant of such faculties may well indicate a pattern for action which other ordinaries will seek to make available in their dioceses when similar needs and exigencies make a demand to which they cannot adequately respond in virtue solely of the faculty which canon 822, § 4, has conferred on them.

---

[34] Pius XI, litterae apostolicae, 30 apr. 1929, n. 8—*AAS*, XXI (1929), 556.

[35] Snee-Clark, *Diocesan Faculties in the United States* (Woodstock, Md.: Woodstock College Press, 1948), p. 60.

CHAPTER XII

THE PRIVILEGE OF THE PORTABLE ALTAR AS CONFERRED BY LAW

Canon 822, § 2: Privilegium *altaris portatilis* vel iure vel indulto Sedis tantum Apostolicae conceditur.

Although the Council of Trent did not legislate a termination of the privilege of the portable altar enjoyed by bishops and their superiors, the laws passed by that Council on the subject of the general use of the portable altar did connote by their tone the end of the unrestricted enjoyment of that privilege by bishops.[1]

From the time of that Council until the operative enactment of the present Code the privilege of the portable altar as possessed by cardinals and bishops was subject to various restrictions, e.g., it was not lawful for a bishop or a cardinal to go to a private home for the purpose of saying Mass.[2]

Although some of these restrictions may still be commendable as prudent safeguards for the eminent dignity of the Holy Sacrifice, they are no longer part of the law in the Code, and hence no longer have an imperative force.

This chapter, which proposes to treat of those on whom the law bestows the privilege of the portable altar, has been opened with a discussion of the privilege enjoyed by bishops and cardinals, for they are the principal recipients of this favor from the general law.

Among the many privileges enjoyed by cardinals is that of celebrating Mass on a portable altar, not only in their own residence, but wherever they may be, and moreover of permitting another priest in their presence to say Mass on the portable altar.[3]

---

[1] Cf. *supra*, pp. 32 ff.

[2] Decr. *Nonnulli*, 15 dec. 1703—*Fontes*, n. 264. Cf. Gasparri, *De Sanctissima Eucharistia*, I, nn. 267, 268.

[3] Can. 239, § 1, n. 7.

This is the content of the law. It will be noted that it is singularly free from restrictions. It allows cardinals to celebrate Mass not only in an unconsecrated or unblessed place, but also in a place not destined for divine worship.[4] As has been shown above, however, the use of a bedroom as a suitable place for Mass now seems to be excluded.[5]

The prohibition found in canon 822, § 3, against the use of the privilege of the portable altar for saying Mass at sea is not applicable to cardinals. For besides their privilege of the portable altar they possess the added one of celebrating aboard ship while traveling at sea. This latter privilege they possess, not in consequence of their privilege of the portable altar, but through a separate and distinct concession made in the Code.[6]

Annexed to the cardinal's personal privilege of celebrating Mass on a portable altar is the faculty of permitting another Mass to be celebrated in his presence. Thus, while the cardinal is making his act of thanksgiving after Mass he can permit some priest to say Mass on his portable altar. This is an added privilege, for normally the granted privilege of the portable altar when possessed by indult is strictly personal, intended solely for the benefit of the priest grantee, and hence cannot be extended to another priest. This extension of the cardinal's privilege is very ancient; it dates from the original grant of Pope Boniface VIII.[7]

This privilege is clearly granted for the convenience of the cardinal both as an aid to his own devotion in celebrating Mass and also as a means whereby he may hear Mass when he is sick and unable to celebrate personally. For the extension to another of his own privilege of celebrating Mass on a portable altar it is not necessary that the cardinal himself celebrate; the wording of

---

[4] Can. 822, §3.

[5] *Supra*, pp. 70, 71.

[6] Can. 236, § 1, n. 8: Cardinales facultate gaudent celebrandi in mari, debitis cautelis adhibitis. Cf. Hynes, *Privileges of Cardinals*, pp. 73–75; Blat, *Commentarium Textus Codicis Iuris Canonici* (5 vols. in 7, Vol. III, pars I [*De Sacramentis*], Romae: Ex Typographia Pontificia in Instituto Pii X, 1924), p. 144.

[7] C. 12, *de privilegiis*, V, 7, in VI°; cf. *supra*, p. 21 ff.

the canon, "*ipsis adstantibus,*" does however make it necessary that the priest say the Mass in the cardinal's presence. The privilege is made available as a personal favor, and hence the cardinal must be present when it is called into use.[8]

Finally, it is certain that any of the faithful who hear Mass which is said on a portable altar, either by the cardinal himself or by some priest in his presence, fulfill the obligation of a preceptive Mass. This was confirmed in 1896 through a decree of the Sacred Congregation of Rites,[9] and this decree, as the authors commonly attest, was not revoked by the Code.[10]

The privilege of the portable altar is enjoyed by the cardinals from the moment the Pope has announced their names to the other cardinals gathered in secret consistory.[11]

Canon 349, § 1, n. 1, states that all bishops, whether residential or titular, enjoy the same privilege of the portable altar as do the cardinals. They begin to enjoy this favor from the moment they have received official notification of their canonical appointment. It may be of interest to point out that, whereas the arrangement of the Code now has the bishops sharing in the privileges of the cardinals, historically just the reverse of this was true.

Notwithstanding the historical background of the question, bishops and cardinals were put on equal footing by the Code as far as the extent and the limitations of their respective privileges of the portable altar are concerned. Hence the bishop can make use of the portable altar outside of his own diocese without seeking permission from the local ordinary. He may also permit that in his presence a second Mass be said on his portable altar by a priest of his choice. At either of these Masses the attending faithful may satisfy the precept of hearing Mass.

---

[8] Coronata, *De Locis et Temporibus Sacris,* pp. 126, 127; Hynes, *Privileges of Cardinals,* pp. 70–73.

[9] S. R. C., *Urbis et Orbis,* 8 iun, 1896—*Fontes,* n. 6261. Cf. *supra,* p. 34.

[10] Cf. Hynes, *Privileges of Cardinals,* p. 73; Cappello, *De Sacramentis,* I, n. 718; Vermeersch-Creusen, *Epitome Iuris Canonici,* II, n. 563; Bouscaren-Ellis, *Canon Law* (Milwaukee, Wis.: Bruce Publishing Co., 1946), p. 630.

[11] Can. 239, § 1; can. 233, § 1.

Other dignitaries on whom the law confers the privilege of the portable altar, albeit in a more restricted manner, are the vicars and prefects apostolic, the apostolic administrators, the protonotaries apostolic "*de numero participantium,*" and the auditors of the Holy Roman Rota.

Canon 308 furnishes the basis on which vicars and prefects apostolic may claim for themselves the privilege of the portable altar.[12] If they possess the episcopal rank, then that very fact constitutes the source of their privilege; but if they are not bishops, they possess the privilege in virtue of their sharing in the privileges of protonotaries apostolic *de numero participantium.* In this latter case, so the canon states, they enjoy the privilege only during their term of office and only when they are within their own territory.

In this connection Bliley [13] calls attention to an error made by Coronata when he stated that vicars and prefects apostolic enjoy the privilege of the portable altar in virtue of the ruling contained in canon 294, § 1.[14] If they are not themselves bishops, then the vicars and prefects apostolic gain the privilege of the portable altar by sharing in the privileges of protonotaries apostolic *de numero participantium,* and not by sharing in the privileges of bishops.

It must be clear from the foregoing discussion that protonotaries apostolic *de numero participantium* enjoy the privilege of the portable altar. This concession is indeed not mentioned in the Code, but its existence long antedates the advent of the Code. In the footnote to canon 308 reference is made to the Motu proprio *Inter multiplices* of Pope Pius X (1903–1914),[15] which stated that with regard to the privilege of the portable altar the regulations as

---

[12] Can. 308: Vicariis et Praefectis, charactere episcopali auctis, privilegia honorifica competunt, quae ius concedit Episcopis titularibus; si autem charactere episcopali careant, habent tantum, durante munere et in proprio territorio, insignia et privilegia Protonotariorum apostolicorum de numero participantium.

[13] *Altars According to the Code,* p. 114.

[14] Coronata, *De Locis et Temporibus Sacris,* p. 126.

[15] Pius X, motu propr., *Inter multiplices,* 21 febr. 1905, n. 2—*Fontes,* n. 665.

set down by Pope Pius IX (1846–1878) in the Constitution *Quamvis peculiaris* were still in force.[16]

This earlier constitution granted the privilege of the portable altar to protonotaries apostolic *de numero participantium,* but with the restriction that it could be used in no other place except the possessor's home unless he was on a journey, or unless he had occasion to employ the privilege for the sake of bestowing a favor upon those good people in whose home he was sojourning. The celebration of only one Mass was permitted, but it could be said either by the grantee himself or by some priest of his choice. This constitution also had set certain limits with reference to those who could fulfill their precept by attending such a Mass; however the later *motu proprio* of Pope Pius X stated that these prelates could rightfully declare that all who attended the Mass thereby fulfilled their obligation of hearing Mass.[17]

There can be no doubt that their privilege remains in effect after the promulgation of the Code. Pius XI confirmed this in 1934.[18]

Protonotaries apostolic *supranumerarii* and *ad instar* did not have this privilege before the Code, nor do they enjoy it now. They do however have the privilege of the domestic oratory.[19]

Permanent apostolic administrators enjoy all the privileges of residential bishops, and hence may use a portable altar in all situations in which a bishop may use one.[20]

If the apostolic administrators are appointed temporarily, then

---

[16] Pius IX, const. *Quamvis peculiaris,* 9 febr. 1853—*Pii IX Pontificis Maximi Acta* (9 vols., Romae: Ex Typographia Bonorum Artium, 1854–1878), I, 413, 414.

[17] Pius X, motu propr., *Inter multiplices,* 21 febr. 1905, n. 11—*Fontes,* n. 665.

[18] Pius XI, const. *Ad incrementum decoris,* 15 aug. 1934, n. XLVI—*AAS,* XXVI (1934), 507.

[19] Pius X, motu propr., *Inter multiplices,* 21 febr. 1905, nn. 22, 46—*Fontes,* n. 665; Pius XI, const. *Ad incrementum decoris,* 1 aug. 1934, nn. LV, LVII—*AAS,* XXVI (1934), 508.

[20] Can. 315, § 1. Cf. McDonough, *Apostolic Administrators,* The Catholic University of America Canon Law Studies, n. 139 (Washington, D. C.: The Catholic University of America Press, 1941), pp. 158 ff.

canon 315, § 2, n. 2, indicates that the possession and use of their privileges are regulated by the ruling contained in canon 308. Hence, if they are bishops, they enjoy the privilege of the portable altar in virtue of that fact.[21] If they are not of episcopal rank, they nevertheless enjoy the use of the portable altar, since that privilege is numbered among the privileges possessed by the protonotaries apostolic *de numero participantium.* Canon law gives apostolic administrators a share in these privileges.[22]

The only practical consequence of the diverse sources of this privilege is that the temporary apostolic administrators who are bishops can permit in their presence another Mass to be said on their portable altar. The temporary apostolic administrators who do not possess the episcopal dignity cannot do this.[23]

The auditors of the Holy Roman Rota enjoyed the privilege of the portable altar before the Code.[24] This privilege was reaffirmed for them in 1934 by Pope Pius XI,[25] who also stated that all who are present at the Mass can fulfill the obligation of a preceptive Mass.

Pope Pius XI in this same constitution also gave the privilege of the portable altar to the following groups of dignitaries: the assessors and secretaries of the Sacred Roman Congregations,[26] the eight prelatial clerics of the Venerable Apostolic Camera,[27] the seven voting prelates or consultants of the Apostolic Signa-

---

[21] Cans. 349, § 1, n. 1; 239, § 1, n. 7.

[22] Cans. 315, § 2, n. 2; 308; McDonough, *Apostolic Administrators,* pp. 113 ff.

[23] The permanent apostolic administrator is not mentioned in this connection, for canon 315, § 1, gives him all the privileges of bishops. As a matter of fact the authors say that a permanent apostolic administrator is always a bishop. Cf. McDonough, *Apostolic Administrators,* p. 162; Wernz-Vidal, *Ius Canonicum* (7 vols. in 8, Vol. II [*De Personis*], 3. ed., 1943, Romae: Apud Aedes Universitatis Gregorianae), II, p. 701, n. 557.

[24] Cf. Wernz, *Ius Decretalium* (3. ed., 6 vols., Prati, 1913–1915), V, n. 85, in nota 53, n. 6; Many, *Praelectiones de Missa* (Parisiis, 1903), p. 17.

[25] Pius XI, const. *Ad incrementum decoris,* 15 aug. 1934, n. LXXIV—*AAS,* XXVI (1934), 511.

[26] Pius XI, const. *Ad incrementum decoris,* 15 aug. 1934, n. XVII—*AAS,* XXVI (1934), 503.

[27] Pius XI, const. *Ad incrementum decoris,* 15 aug. 1934, n. CVIII—*AAS,* XXVI (1934), 515.

tura,[28] and the referendary prelates or reporters of the Apostolic Signatura.[29]

All other privileges which allow the use of a portable altar are held in virtue of a special indult from the Holy See. Cappello adds, to the list of those who are mentioned above, such as are abbots and prelates *nullius*. It is his opinion that canon 323 grants to these two groups the privileges of residential bishops.[30]

While this canon confers the ordinary episcopal powers on abbots and prelates *nullius*, and likewise imposes on them the episcopal obligations, it nowhere mentions episcopal privileges. It consequently does not seem to justify an assertion that abbots and prelates *nullius* enjoy the privilege of the portable altar.

Benko[31] noted that while canon 349 extended many privileges to the bishop, these could in no way be appropriated by the abbot *nullius* because the grants of canon 349, § 1, n. 1, are made to the bishops *personally*.[32]

Other than the above-mentioned dignitaries there is no one on whom the law confers the privilege of the portable altar.

---

[28] Pius XI, const. *Ad incrementum decoris*, 15 aug. 1934, n. CXXVII, d —*AAS*, XXVI (1934), 518.

[29] Pius XI, const. *Ad incrementum decoris*, 15 aug. 1934, n. CXLV—*AAS*, XXVI (1934), 520.

[30] Cappello, *De Sacramentis*, I, n. 718, p. 676. Wernz-Vidal also enumerate them among those who have the privilege, but do not offer any specific commentary—*Ius Canonicum*, Tom. IV, Vol. I (Romae: Apud Aedes Universitatis Gregorianae, 1934), p. 117.

[31] *The Abbot Nullius*, The Catholic University of America Canon Law Studies, n. 173 (Washington, D. C.: The Catholic University of America Press, 1943), p. 115.

[32] Cf. Bliley, *Altars According to the Code*, p. 114.

CHAPTER XIII

THE PRIVILEGE OF THE PORTABLE ALTAR AS CONFERRED BY INDULT

Article One: The Privilege as Enjoyed by Religious

From the very title of this chapter it is clear that the Code offers no direct or specific legislation on the matter here treated. Accordingly the present discussion does not relate to the universal law in so far as it provides for the use of the portable altar, but rather to the particular indults by means of which the Holy See grants the privilege of the portable altar. The law of the Code will, however, be taken into consideration in so far as it legislates concerning indults and privileges in general, and regarding the manner in which they are shared by means of a reciprocal participation in the original grant.

The remarks made and the conclusions drawn in Chapter Seven concerning the privilege of the portable altar as it was enjoyed by religious after the Council of Trent are still applicable to the present situation, for the Code did not work any change in these privileges, nor did it put an end to papal privileges which had been granted before the promulgation of the Code.

It here seems warranted briefly to sum up what was said in Chapter Seven: the Council of Trent completely abolished the widespread use of the portable altar by religious. However, Popes who reigned subsequently to that Council made new grants of this same privilege in a more limited field.[1] These new grants were indeed very limited, both in their content and in the number of those who enjoyed them. Yet the practical consequence of this fact was not as far-reaching as it may appear to have been, since the increased occurrence of the reciprocal participation in granted privileges, as it then obtained among the religious, made the enjoyment of many granted privileges possible among a very extended number of persons.

[1] Cf. Bliley, *Altars According to the Code,* p. 116.

In Chapter Eight the effect of this institute on the privilege of the portable altar was outlined at some length. It will suffice here to repeat the conclusion as there established, namely, that almost all religious appeared to enjoy the use of the portable altar when they were actively engaged in mission work.[2]

This state of affairs remained unchanged until the advent of the Code in 1918. At that time the authors were thrown into great confusion on the topic of the intercommunication of privileges. This confusion was occasioned by the clause incorporated in canon 613, § 1: "*exclusa in posterum qualibet communicatione.*" In the minds of many this clause raised a doubt whether the law implied that the privileges which had been acquired in the past by way of a mutual sharing in the original grant were thenceforth to be considered as abrogated, or whether the law simply insisted that for the future no new privileges could be acquired by means of reciprocal participation among religious.[3]

The far-reaching consequences of these divergent opinions occasioned a lively debate until the Holy See decided the issue. This definition came in 1938 from the Pontifical Commission for the Interpretation of the Code, but it had been foreshadowed in an earlier grant which Pope Pius XI made to the Jesuits. In this document, issued in 1933, the Pope confirmed all the pre-Code privileges as enjoyed by the Society of Jesus, and in so doing he also made explicit mention of those privileges which the Jesuits had gained through their sharing in privileges that had directly been granted to others.[4]

This decree of the Pope undoubtedly paved the way for the later response of the Pontifical Commission when there was proposed to it the following *dubium*:

> An verba canonis 613, § 1, "exclusa in posterum qualibet communicatione," ita intelligenda sint ut revocata fuerint privilegia a religionibus ante Codicem Iuris Canonici per communicationem legitime acquisita et pacifice possessa.

[2] *Supra,* p. 49. Cf. Matulenas, *Communication, A Source of Privilege,* pp. 121 ff.

[3] Matulenas, *op. cit.,* p. 126.

[4] Pius XI, *Paterna caritas,* 12 mart. 1933—*AAS,* XXV (1933), 245.

The response was given in the negative, so that it is now clear that the Code did not abrogate the privileges of which religious had gained rightful possession through the acknowledged means of inter-participation as it obtained before the present Code.[5]

Since the Code brought no changes in the privilege of the portable altar as enjoyed by religious, and the commentary already given on the pre-Code law is still applicable, it can be said that religious in general enjoy the use of a portable altar while they are engaged in mission work. What added grants any individual institutes may have by way of special indult from the Holy See can best be discovered through an inquiry directed to the superior of the institute in question.

Article Two: The Privilege as Enjoyed by Members of the Missionary Union of the Clergy and Other Organizations

Since the time of the reorganization of the whole system of the Third Orders Secular by Pope Leo XIII, it is no longer possible for secular priests to obtain the privilege of the portable altar through membership in the Third Order of any religious institute.[6]

Although that avenue of obtaining the privilege is now closed, there are still several means which served either in the immediate past, or which serve even in the present, to make available for priests the enjoyment of the privilege of the portable altar.

Among the spiritual favors granted to perpetual and special members of the Missionary Union of the Clergy during a five year period from August 1936 to August 1941 was the privilege of the portable altar for a priest member on vacation, which privilege was to be used with the consent of the priest's own ordinary, without prejudice to the rights of pastors, and on condition that the altar was erected in a decent and suitable place. Special members of the Missionary Union enjoyed this privilege only during the above-mentioned five year period, but priests who became perpetual members before August of 1941 enjoy the use

[5] Responsum P.C.I., 30 dec. 1937—*AAS,* XXX (1938), 73. Cf. Goyenche, "Commentarium in Responsum ad Can. 613, § 1," *Apollinaris* (Romae, 1928–), XI (1938), 178–180. There he gives an excellent history of the controversy.

[6] *Supra,* p. 50.

of the portable altar in perpetuity under the terms of the privilege.[7]

The wording of the privilege, "*tempore vacationum,*" limits its use to an actual vacation time. However, nothing is specified about the duration of the vacation, and there is no reason to doubt that the privilege can be employed when the priest is away for but a few days. This privilege cannot be enjoyed at home during a time of infirm health or convalescence, but an independent privilege for use under these conditions can be obtained, as will be shown presently. If a priest is at his family's home on vacation, he can doubtless use the privilege of the portable altar which he enjoys through his membership in the Missionary Union of the Clergy. The circumstances under which a man chooses to spend his vacation are not regulated by the grant, provided only that Mass is said in a decent place.

This privilege of using the portable altar on vacations requires the permission of the priest's own ordinary, but not the permission of the ordinary of the place if the priest chances to be vacationing outside of his own diocese. If the priest is in good standing and is legitimately on vacation, the permission of his bishop can very probably be presumed.

The provision in the privilege that the rights of local pastors must never be violated probably envisions the case in which a vacationing priest's celebration of Mass for a group of his friends would preclude their attendance at the parish Masses, so that in consequence thereof the local parish church would sustain a loss in revenue. There need be no fear on this score if the priest vacationer restricts the number of those who attend his Mass to the circle of his immediate friends and relatives, and if at the same time he prudently reminds them that their financial obligations to the local parish, whatever they may be, are not suspended. A little consideration for the good order and welfare of

[7] Privileges granted to Special and Perpetual Members of the Missionary Union of the Clergy in the United States of America by His Holiness, Pope Pius XI, at the request of His Excellency, the Most Reverend Amleto Giovanni Cicognani, Archbishop of Laodicea, and Apostolic Delegate to the United States, in an audience on August 22, 1936. This grant is found in the brochure of privileges issued by the Missionary Union of the Clergy.

the parish in which he is staying will serve both to safeguard the law and to advance the cause of religion.

No other limitations are placed on this privilege of the portable altar except that which amounts to a restatement of the natural law, namely, that Mass must be said in a decent and suitable place. The remarks made in Chapter Nine[8] on this limitation are also applicable here. Moreover, the Instruction of the Sacred Congregation of the Sacraments, *Quam plurimum,* which condemns a bedroom as being an unsuitable place for offering Mass, seems also to be applicable to the privileges under discussion here.[9]

Although the use of the privilege treated above is limited to those times when a priest is on vacation, membership in the Catholic Near East Welfare Association accords another very useful privilege of the portable altar. All perpetual and annual members of the Catholic Near East Welfare Association enrolled before April 21, 1945, and all who become perpetual members thereafter, enjoy the privilege of the portable altar for the celebration of Mass at home during a time of infirm health or convalescence.

Unlike the privilege to use a portable altar while one is vacationing, the present privilege for saying Mass at home during an illness can still be obtained by priests who join the Catholic Near East Welfare Association.[10]

The privilege is restricted to the use of a portable altar at home. No violence would seem to be done to this restriction if a priest said Mass in his rectory, or in his own or his family's home. The use of the word " home " in the indult does however seem definitely to exclude the use of the privilege while a priest is confined to a hospital. If the priest by reason of old age or infirmity is living in some sort of home for the aged or infirm, it seems that he can avail himself of the privilege, for such an institution is really his home at the time.

One can scarcely indicate any definite or exact rule for determining the precise meaning of infirmity and convalescence. The common estimation of men will be a safe guide for the priest's

---

[8] *Supra,* pp. 56 ff.

[9] S. C. de Sacramentis, instr. *Quam plurimum,* 1 oct. 1949, II, 9, a—*AAS,* XLI (1949), 504. Cf. *supra,* pp. 60 ff.

[10] Cf. *Faculties, Privileges and Indulgences,* n. 1—Catholic Near East Welfare Association, New York.

own conscience in determining whether or not in a given set of circumstances he is free to avail himself of the privilege of the portable altar.

Other privileges of a similar nature which are granted from time to time by the Holy See through various organizations in the Church must be interpreted in the light of the general principles already stated, as well as within the limitations contained in the indults themselves.

Finally, mention should be made of the faculty which at present the Apostolic Delegate can grant in regard to the portable altar. Faculty number 36 includes the power of granting, as often as necessity urges and there is not sufficient time for recourse to the Holy See, an indult, in particular cases, of celebrating Mass outside a church or oratory, and of erecting an altar in the open air. Also the Apostolic Delegate can under the same conditions grant to priests who travel over water, whether on the ocean or on rivers, the faculty of celebrating Mass on board ship on a portable altar, provided that the place is decent and suitable, and provided also that there is no danger of the spilling of the Precious Blood.[11]

Article Three: The Privilege as Enjoyed by Chaplains of the Armed Forces

To celebrate Mass in a respectable and decent place, even in the open and aboard ship, for a just cause and avoiding all danger of irreverence.[12]

In accordance with the Holy See's policy of supplying military chaplains with very wide powers for the more efficacious discharge of their office, the privilege of the portable altar as conferred on them is almost without limitation. For any just cause they may set up a portable altar and say Mass in any decent and safe place whatsoever. A just cause is demanded by the wording of the faculty, but not a grave one. Moreover, while the saying of Mass at sea is generally excluded from granted privileges of the portable

---

[11] *Faculties (Private)*, c. IV, nn. 36, 37—Bouscaren, *Canon Law Digest*, I, 182.

[12] *Facultates Castrenses ad Usum Cappellanorum Copiis Armatis Statuum Foederatorum Americae Septentrionalis Addictorum* (3. ed., 1948), pars II: *Facultates pro Tempore Belli Concessae*, sectio I, 2. Cf. Bouscaren, *Canon Law Digest*, II, 607.

altar, it is expressly included in this grant to chaplains of the armed forces. This is quite understandable if one considers that the exigencies of modern warfare necessarily involve large naval forces as well as transportation by sea of large land forces. Chaplains of such troops must certainly be permitted to offer Mass at sea if they are to fulfill their appointed office successfully.

It is also expressly stated that chaplains may celebrate Mass in chapels that are assigned to the armed forces, even if these chapels have not been reserved exclusively for Catholics.[13]

A further concession in favor of military chaplains was made during the late war when permission was granted to chaplains to offer Mass without a portable altar, as long as they used instead a veil containing some relics authenticated by a bishop.[14]

Many chaplains availed themselves of this privilege by using a Greek Antimensium. This practice is certainly within the limits of the faculty, and indeed reflects the most practical solution, but if any bishop would authenticate some relics and these would be safely inserted in a veil, a chaplain could certainly say Mass on such a veil. The wording of the faculty makes this evident beyond doubt.

---

[13] *Facultates castrenses,* pars I: *Facultates Habituales Vicariatus Castrensis,* n. 3. Cf. Bouscaren, *Canon Law Digest,* II, 588.

[14] A response given on February 26, 1943, by the Sacred Congregation of Rites, Prot. num. 2628/43, to the Military Vicar, Francis Cardinal Spellman:

Beatissime Pater,

R. P. D. Franciscus J. Spellman Archiepiscopus Neo Eboracensis et Ordinarius Castrensis pro America Septentrionali ad pedes Sanctitatis Vestrae provolutus privilegium implorat pro cappellanis castrensibus utendi loco altaris portatilis in celebratione Missae, velo cum inclusis Reliquiis ab Episcopo recognitis.

Ordinariatus Militaris Americae Septentrionalis.

Sanctissimus Dominus Noster Pius Papa XII preces Excellentissimi

Ordinarii Militaris Americae Septentrionalis ab infrascripto Cardinali Sacrae Rituum Congregationis Praefecto relatas peramanter excipiens, benigne annuere pro gratia iuxta preces dignatus est, servatis de cetero servandis in celebratione Missae. Contrariis non obstantibus quibuscumque. Die 26 Februarii 1943.

Carolus Card. Salotti
S. R. C. Praefectus

CHAPTER XIV

THE SUNDAY PRECEPT AND THE PORTABLE ALTAR

The portable altar and its relationship with the precept of hearing Mass can probably best be discussed under a twofold heading. The first consideration is whether or not the precept of hearing Mass can be fulfilled by attendance at Mass offered on a portable altar. The second question is whether or not there exists an obligation to attend a Mass offered on a portable altar when that is the only means possible for the satisfying of a preceptive Mass.

On the first point the Code of Canon Law is silent. The legislation on the place in which the precept of hearing Mass can be fulfilled is found in canon 1249. That canon reads:

> **Legi de audiendo Sacro satisfacit qui Missae adest quocumque catholico ritu celebretur, sub dio aut in quacumque ecclesia vel oratorio publico aut semi-publico et in privatis coemeteriorum aediculis de quibus in can. 1190, non vero in aliis oratoriis privatis, nisi hoc privilegium a Sede Apostolica concessum fuerit.**

The canon states that the precept of hearing Mass *can* be fulfilled by means of an attendance at the Holy Sacrifice offered "*sub dio,*" or in any church, or public or semi-public oratory, or in private oratories erected in cemeteries. Canon 1249 continues that the precept of hearing Mass *cannot* be fulfilled through attendance at Mass said in any other private oratory, except by way of special privilege. It is to be noted that no direct mention is made of the portable altar. The canon declares that in certain places the precept of hearing Mass can be fulfilled, and that in others it cannot. Neither list is said to be all-inclusive, and neither list includes any mention of the portable altar. However, there is mention of Mass said "*sub dio,*" which must necessarily involve the use of a portable altar. The implications of this implicit mention will be explored at this juncture.

As was noted previously, the expression "*sub dio*" has been understood by Beste[1] to mean simply "*ubivis.*" He does not pursue the matter any further, but apparently it is his understanding that the Code uses this expression "*sub dio*" as a generic phrase under which it would embrace all occasions on which Mass is said on a portable altar. At first examination this appears to be an entirely gratuitous assertion, yet closer inspection will show that the claim is not without advantages. It may here be noted that canon 1249 offers the only legislation in the Code on the place for the fulfillment of the precept of hearing Mass. It can, then, be justifiably considered as legislating for all general possibilities. It does in fact mention churches, and public, semi-public and private oratories. There remains but one possibility, the portable altar, and the canon mentions but one more locale, Mass said "*sub dio.*" Any attempt to reconcile the two elements does seem to enjoy the weight of logic.

Besides the foregoing argument which can be said to be intrinsic to canon 1249, another argument can be advanced in support of the generic interpretation of the phrase "*sub dio.*" This argument is based on the power given to the bishop by canon 822, § 4, to permit the saying of Mass on a portable altar for a just and reasonable cause in an extraordinary case and *per modum actus.*[2] This canon does not limit the use of the faculty to the granting of permission for the celebrating of Mass "*sub dio*"; when in virtue of the faculty due permission has been granted, the Mass may be celebrated in a safe and decent place. Nowhere in the Code is the bishop given the power to legislate concerning the place for the fulfillment of the precept of hearing Mass. Therefore unless the phrase "*sub dio*" of canon 1249 means any place in which a portable altar may be used, it does not seem clear how

[1] *Introductio in Codicem,* p. 620.

[2] Can. 822, § 4: Loci Ordinarius aut, si agatur de domo religionis exemptae, Superior maior, licentiam celebrandi extra ecclesiam et oratorium super petram sacram et decenti loco, numquam autem in cubiculo, concedere potest iusta ac rationabili de causa, in aliquo extraordinario casu et per modum actus.

the people who attend Mass which is said on a portable altar by virtue of the bishop's power under canon 822, § 4, can thereby fulfill the obligation of a preceptive Mass.

Coronata,[3] like Beste, maintained that anyone who heard Mass when it was celebrated on a portable altar could thereby fulfill the precept of hearing Mass, unless the indult in virtue of which the portable altar was used had stated otherwise, or the Mass was said in a private oratory. He did not state this apodictically; rather, he employed the expression "*ni fallor.*" He argued that canon 1249 contains but a single exception regarding the place where the precept of hearing Mass can be fulfilled; that exception refers, not to the privilege of the portable altar, but to strictly private oratories alone. He then concluded that the precept could be fulfilled in any place in which the privilege of the portable altar is used.

In corroboration of this argument he said that many authors under the earlier law had taught that the precept of hearing Mass prescribed only the hearing of Mass without any determination of place, and that therefore the precept could be fulfilled in any place whatsoever. The Code, then, merely determined the place in so far as it excluded the private oratory. Therefore, he concluded, under the present law the precept of hearing Mass can be fulfilled in any place whatsoever outside of churches, wherever the Mass is celebrated in virtue of the privilege of the portable altar, with the single exception of the private oratory. Of course, if the indult which granted the privilege of the portable altar expressly stated otherwise, its ruling would have to be followed.

Against these arguments others of perhaps greater force can be advanced. For while it is true that the generic interpretation by which "*sub dio*" is understood to mean "*ubivis*" does seem very logical and does solve certain problems, yet it creates other difficulties. If the legislator meant that the precept of hearing Mass could be fulfilled anywhere except in a private oratory, then it seems logical to expect that he would have said that, and not have had recourse to the enumeration of all the possibilities, especially in equivocal language.

In regard to canon 822, § 4, and its relationship to the precept

[3] *De Locis et Temporibus Sacris*, nn. 123, 190.

of hearing Mass, while it is indeed true that the simplest solution could be had in the case that the precept of hearing Mass could be fulfilled at any Mass said on a portable altar, still another and an adequate solution of this problem can be provided even though one does not admit that the phrase "*sub dio*" of canon 1249 means everywhere but in a private oratory.

This explanation has its basis in canon 66, § 3, which states that when a faculty is granted it includes all other powers which are necessary for its use.[4] As has been shown previously,[5] the most common reason for which the bishop would permit Mass on a portable altar outside a church would be to enable the faithful to fulfill the precept of hearing Mass when they otherwise could not do so. If this is a customary purpose of the granting of this privilege, then by virtue of canon 66, § 3, the bishop must have the power to dispense from the law of canon 1249, which deals with the permissible places in which the fulfillment of the Sunday precept can be properly achieved.

This line of argumentation is ably presented by Guiniven.[6] To forestall a possible objection he pointed out that the power of dispensing from the common law can be granted *implicitly* by the Code inasmuch as canon 81 states:

> **A generalibus Ecclesiae legibus Ordinarii infra Romanum Pontificem dispensare nequeunt . . . nisi haec potestas eisdem fuerit explicite vel implicite concessa. . . .**

Canon 63, § 3, certainly seems to point to an example of an implicit grant of the power to dispense from the law of the prescribed place for hearing Mass.

Another objection that Guiniven has answered is that the authority which is granted to ordinaries by canon 822, § 4, does not connote a "faculty" as contemplated in canon 66, § 3, but rather the presence of ordinary power, and that therefore canon

[4] Can. 66, § 3: Concessa facultas secumfert alias quoque potestates quae ad illius usum sunt necessariae; . . . .

[5] *Supra*, pp. 73 ff.

[6] *The Precept of Hearing Mass*, pp. 124 ff.

66, § 3, is not applicable.[7] It is true, he said, that the power which bishops enjoy to allow Mass to be celebrated outside of churches and oratories is ordinary power. However, since there is no express provision of law with regard to special powers granted to an office by the Code (ordinary power), it seems safe to proceed according to the prescriptions of canon 20, which states:

> **Si certa de re desit expressum praescriptum legis . . . norma sumenda est . . . a legibus latis in similibus.**

The power granted to bishops as ordinary power in canon 822, § 4, corresponds to the similar, though more extensive, power usually granted to ordinaries in the Apostolic Faculties. Canon 66, § 3, is applicable to the Apostolic Faculties, and therefore, by reason of canon 20, would also seem to be applicable to the power as granted in canon 822, § 4.

Treating of a practical case of the bishop's use of the power given him by canon 822, § 4, Bastnagel has stated that the purpose of the grant is to make attendance at Mass possible under circumtances which abstract from the normal requirements of the law regarding the place of celebration. It appears then to follow quite naturally that the grant also contemplates that the Sunday obligation will be fulfilled under the circumstances in which the hearing of Mass is rendered possible.[8] The fact that the author found it necessary to adopt this line of explanation seems to establish the fact that he is not of the opinion that the precept of hearing Mass can be ordinarily fulfilled by attendance at the Holy Sacrifice when offered on a portable altar.

Against the argument advanced by Coronata that the pre-Code law permitted the precept of hearing Mass to be fulfilled anywhere, and that the Code has merely limited that to exclude the possibility of hearing a preceptive Mass in a private oratory, the writer has already noted in an earlier connection that this line of argumentation presupposes that the phrase "*sub dio*" of canon 1249 must be understood in a very wide sense, as tantamount in fact to some

---

[7] Guiniven, *op. cit.*, pp. 125, 126.

[8] Bastnagel, "Cases and Studies," *The Jurist,* II (1942), 157.

expression that would mean everywhere.[9] In the previous discussion the writer has attempted to show that Coronata's line of argument involves him in a *petitio principii,* for by assuming the wide meaning of "*sub dio*" he is taking for granted the very point that needs to be proved. His appeal to pre-Code authors, being based on the same argument, seems to fail likewise. Since these matters have been treated already,[10] they need not be repeated here.

Bouscaren [11] made a detailed study of this question. Among twenty canonists and moralists whom he consulted, he found only two who treated the matter.

Prümmer (1866–1931) [12] merely stated that, when by some special permission Mass is said in a profane place, all those for whose benefit the permission was granted can then fulfill the precept of hearing Mass. He advanced no arguments in support of this opinion.

Genicot (1856–1900)-Salsmans (1873–1944) [13] were the other authors who treated the matter. They said that the precept is satisfied by all who attend Mass said "*sub dio*" . . . or in general when Mass is said in a place that is not altogether private, by permission of the Ordinary or by a privilege that is not merely personal. By the reference to a privilege that is not merely personal, the authors probably had in mind a privilege such as that which is enjoyed by military chaplains.

After his own study of the question, Bouscaren [14] found himself in agreement with the above-mentioned authors. He found that prior to the Code it was generally accepted among commentators that the precept of hearing Mass could be fulfilled in any place in which the bishop legitimately permitted Mass to be said.[15]

---

[9] *Supra,* pp. 58 ff.

[10] *Supra,* p. 58.

[11] De Missa ex licentia Ordinarii celebrata," *Periodica,* XXVIII (1939), 52–61.

[12] *Manuale Theologiae Moralis* (5. ed., 3 vols., Friburgi Brisgoviae: Herder & Co., 1928), II, n. 482.

[13] *Institutiones Theologiae Moralis* (13. ed., 2 vols., Bruxellis: Edition Universelle, 1936), I, n. 342.

[14] "Art. cit.," p. 53.

[15] Cf. Gattico, *De Oratoriis Domesticis et de Usu Altaris Portatilis,* cap. XV, n. 5; Many, *De Missa,* n. 6.

The Code, he argued, seems to have continued this doctrine implicitly, for canon 822 has been declared by the Sacred Congregation of the Sacraments to confirm the old law.[16]

Bouscaren expressly remarked that he was treating only of the case in which the local ordinary in virtue of canon 822, § 4, has permitted the saying of Mass outside of a church. He was not treating of Mass said "*sub dio,*" or of Mass said by virtue of a purely personal privilege of the portable altar. From this statement alone it is not possible to get a clear picture of his opinion on whether or not the precept of hearing Mass can be satisfied through attendance at Mass said on a portable altar. Yet here too his whole line of argumentation seems to indicate that he does not subscribe to the opinion that attendance at Mass said on a portable altar always satisfies the precept. Indeed, in his recently published commentary on the Code, while treating of canon 1249, Bouscaren expressly states that he does not agree with the aforementioned opinion of Coronata that Mass said *anywhere* on a portable altar would lend itself as a means for the preceptive hearing of Mass.[17]

It is interesting to note that Bouscaren, by pursuing the same line of argumentation as in the case given above, concluded that attendance even at a Mass said in a private oratory by virtue of a special permission given by the ordinary suffices for the satisfying of the precept of hearing Mass. His attempts to reconcile this view with canon 1249 do not seem to be entirely successful.[18]

Another argument that can be advanced against those who defend the position that the precept of hearing Mass can be fulfilled by attendance at any Mass said on a portable altar outside of a private oratory is based on the special privileges accorded to cardinals, bishops, and others with regard to the portable altar.

The argument is this: The Sacred Congregation of Rites declared in 1896 that any of the faithful who heard Mass which was said on a portable altar, either by a cardinal himself or by

[16] S. C. de Sacramentis, litt. ad Rev.mos Ordinarios Italiae, 26 iul. 1924—*AAS*, XVI (1924), 370.

[17] Bouscaren-Ellis, *Canon Law*, p. 629.

[18] Bouscaren, "De Missa ex licentia Ordinarii celebrata," *Periodica*, XXVIII (1939), pp. 58 ff.

some priest in his presence, fulfilled the obligation of a preceptive Mass.[19] Authors commonly agree that this decree was not revoked by the Code.[20] If the present law permitted the fulfillment of a preceptive Mass whenever Mass is said on a portable altar *any-where* and by anyone possessed of the privilege of the portable altar, it would be pointless for the authors to mention that this old decree is still in force.

An even stronger argument along the same lines can be advanced in the question of the privilege of the portable altar enjoyed by such dignitaries as protonotaries apostolic *de numero partici-pantium* and by the auditors of the Holy Roman Rota, to take but two examples. In 1934 Pope Pius XI confirmed the privileges of these various groups of dignitaries.[21] In connection with the privilege of the portable altar, explicit mention was made in each case that those who attended Mass said on a portable altar by these dignitaries fulfilled thereby their obligation to hear Mass.[22]

The repetition of this added privilege in every instance is certainly without reason or justification if attendance at Mass said by any priest on a portable altar suffices for the fulfillment of the obligation of hearing Mass. The warranted conclusion seems to be that such is not the case, namely that the use of the ordinary privilege of the portable altar does not supply a means whereby the precept of hearing Mass can be fulfilled. The fulfillment of the precept of hearing Mass, when done at Mass said on a portable altar, is rather an unusual occurrence, and the result of a special privilege not contained in the privilege of the portable altar.

From these positive arguments as well as from those propounded in refutation of the opinion of Coronata, it seems better to conclude that Mass said in virtue of a privilege of the portable altar is not in and by itself a suitable occasion for the fulfillment of the preceptive Mass. This must be understood in the sense that the portable altar does not receive mention in canon 1249 as a place

---

19 S. R. C., *Urbis et Orbis,* 8 iun. 1896—*Fontes,* n. 626; can. 239, § 1, 7o.

20 *Supra,* p. 83.

21 Pius XI, const. *Ad incrementum decoris,* 15 aug. 1934, nn. XLVI, LXXIV—*AAS,* XXVI (1934), pp. 507, 511.

22 Cf. *supra,* pp. 84 ff. There a complete list of the dignitaries enjoying this privilege is given.

where always and under all circumstances the obligation of a preceptive Mass can be fulfilled. There is no necessary connection between the portable altar and preceptive Mass except when Mass is said "*sub dio.*"

Moreover the recent Instruction of the Sacred Congregation of the Sacraments, *Quam plurimum,*[23] shows definitely that the above opinion reflects clearly the mind of the Holy See in this regard. In order to forestall abuses, the Congregation said, the Holy See is accustomed to state in the indult granting the privilege of the portable altar whether it also avails those who attend a Mass said in virtue of the privilege with an occasion for fulfilling the precept of hearing Mass. But if, continued the Congregation, express mention of this point is not made in the indult, then the words of Gattico[24] must be taken as the norm. It was his view that those in attendance at a Mass said in virtue of a privilege of the portable altar do not thereby fulfill the precept of hearing Mass unless the privilege is *expressly* extended to them.

The Congregation concluded its discussion of this point by alluding to the statement made in can. 1249 that the Sunday precept may be fulfilled by attendance at a Mass said "*sub dio.*"

While this Instruction nowhere revokes or amends faculties already possessed, its directives do express general and guiding principles and hence seem to be applicable to any such existing grants at least as regards the place and circumstance of using the privilege of the portable altar. Wherefore in view of the Instruction the opinion of Coronata and the others no longer seems probable, namely, that Mass said in virtue of any privilege of the portable altar offers automatically to those in attendance a means of fulfilling the Sunday precept.[25]

The broad outline of the problem having been traced, it will perhaps be useful to delve into specific cases and situations in order to determine what procedure is to be followed if the law is to be preserved from abuse, and if at the same time people are to

[23] S. C. de Sacramentis, instr. *Quam plurimum,* 1 oct. 1949, II, 8—*AAS,* XLI (1949), 504.

[24] *De Oratoriis Domesticis et de Usu Altaris Portatilis,* cap. XV, n. 14.

[25] Cf. Donnelly, "Indults for Portable Altar and Mass Without Server," *The Homiletic and Pastoral Review,* L (1950), 363-364.

be accorded every rightful opportunity for fulfilling their obligation with regard to hearing Mass on Sundays and holy days.

As has been indicated in the course of the preceding argumentation, the privilege of the portable altar as conferred by the law on cardinals, bishops and others carries with it the added privilege that those who attend such Masses fulfill the obligation of hearing Mass.[26] All those present, then, at a Mass said on a portable altar by any one of these dignitaries fulfill thereby their obligation and, moreover, this privilege also avails in connection with the one Mass said in the presence of the bishop or the cardinal on his portable altar.

What if Mass is said in an auditorium, a theatre, or some similar structure, when a parish lacks adequate facilities to care for all its parishioners in a church? Such places cannot be classed as semi-public oratories, for the definition of an oratory demands a "*locus divino cultui destinatus.*" [27]

Since they cannot be classed as semi-public oratories, they do not under canon 1249 fall within the enumeration of the places where the precept may be fulfilled. However, it has been shown that the reason for saying Mass under such circumstances is to enable the people to fulfill their obligation of hearing Mass. Therefore whether Mass is said under such circumstances as a temporary expedient in consequence of the grant of the local ordinary as warranted by canon 822, § 4, or by way of a standing permission derived through a papal indult, those who are in attendance can fulfill their obligation.[28] This doctrine is clearly established and supported by the authority of the commentators.[29] But what is to be said when the situation that prevails directly contravenes the law? It has been noted in the present discussion that canon 822, § 4, makes available for the local ordinary only a *per modum actus* power to permit the celebration of Mass outside of churches. If the situation has existed for some time or it is foreseen that it will continue to exist for some time in the future, two methods of action were suggested: The bishop should either

---

[26] Cf. *supra,* pp. 83 ff.

[27] Can. 1188, § 1.

[28] Cf. *supra,* p .97.

[29] Cf. Guiniven, *The Precept of Hearing Mass,* pp. 122 ff.

delegate his power to the pastor so that the latter can again and again act *per modum actus,* or the bishop should petition Rome for a special indult to cover the emergency. If neither is done, do the people nevertheless continue to fulfill their obligation of hearing Mass by attending the Holy Sacrifice when it is offered under such circumstances?

The writer submits that, since canon 822, § 4, does not give the bishop the power to permit the celebration of Mass in such circumstances, that canon cannot be alleged as a basis on which to rest his claim for the power to dispense from the proper place for the perceptive hearing of Mass. Canon 822, § 4, is said to contain implicitly a dispensation from the proper place for hearing Mass, but if in a given set of circumstances the bishop cannot lawfully use canon 822, § 4, then no other source is open to him whence he can derive the power to dispense from the proper place for the preceptive hearing of Mass. When Mass is being said unlawfully outside a church, then the people who attend that Mass do not thereby succeed objectively in the fulfillment of the precept.

In all of these cases the author is following the stricter opinion, namely that of itself the portable altar is not universally constituted as a suitable place for the fulfillment of the Sunday precept. In the case just examined there seems no room for a divergent opinion, for the precise point at issue was the illicit use of the privilege. Those who maintain that the hearing of Mass when it is offered on a portable altar anywhere suffices for satisfying the precept all presuppose that the privilege is used lawfully.

Regarding the question of the fulfillment of the precept of hearing Mass when the celebration of it is undertaken on shipboard, no doubt remains if the Mass is said in an oratory. Whether the ship's oratory is truly a public oratory or only a semi-public oratory is of no moment, for in either case the precept of hearing Mass can be fulfilled.

If the Mass on board ship is said "*sub dio,*" it is also clear that those in attendance can fulfill the preceptive Mass.[30] In this connection Bouscaren-Ellis [31] stated that if Mass is said on board ship

[30] Can. 1249. Cf. Van Hove, *Tractatus de Sanctissima Eucharistia* (2. ed., Mechliniae: Dessain, 1941), p. 376.

[31] *Canon Law,* p. 629.

in an accessible place, that circumstance can be considered as morally the equivalent of the case in which the altar is set up in the open, and hence the obligation of the preceptive Mass can be fulfilled.

A similar view was taken by Vermeersch (1858–1936). He said that "*sub dio*" simply points to a public place, and that therefore the precept of hearing Mass can be fulfilled by people when they attend at a Mass that is said on a portable altar in some public place on board ship.[32]

These opinions while giving a broad interpretation to the phrase "*sub dio,*" do not in any way support the view that attendance at a Mass which is said in an ordinary stateroom on shipboard proves equally feasible for the purpose in hand. A passenger's private stateroom can hardly be classed as a public place, and consequently when Mass is said therein it cannot be regarded morally as offered "*sub dio.*" Unless the indult which grants the use of the portable altar at sea states otherwise, those who attend Mass said by a priest in his stateroom do not fulfill the precept.[33]

On the topic of offering Mass in a stateroom the Sacred Congregation for the Propagation of the Faith issued a decree in 1902 that seemed to forbid it entirely as being an unsuitable location; but a *dubium* issued a few months later said that it was not the intention of the Sacred Congregation to forbid absolutely and entirely the saying of Mass in private staterooms aboard ship, but rather to insist on the precautions for the safety and reverence due to the Blessed Sacrament that were, in all too many cases, lacking when Mass was offered under such circumstances.[34]

If the Mass is said in an accessible place on board ship, then it is likely that those who are in attendance can fulfill the precept.[35]

On the question of Mass said on a portable altar by virtue of a

---

[32] Vermeersch, "Dubia quaedam de ritibus missae, de praecepto audiendi missam, de praesentia in ordinatione," *Periodica,* XVI (1927), pp. 266*–279*. Cf. Vermeersch-Creusen, *Epitome Iuris Canonici,* II, n. 563.

[33] Genicot-Salsmans, *Institutiones theologiae moralis,* I, n. 342.

[34] S. C. de Prop. Fide, 1 martii, 1902, *Decretum—AAS,* XXXV (1902), 48; S. C. de Prop. Fide, 13 aug. 1902, *Dubium—AAS,* XXXV (1902), 612.

[35] Cf. Regatillo, *Ius Sacramentarium,* I, n. 223; Jombart, "De obligatione audiendi missam in mari," *Periodica,* XIX (1930), 126*.

personal privilege, Regatillo made a twofold distinction which seems to offer a key for the solution of the problem here discussed.[36] He divided the holders of the privilege of the portable altar into two classes: Those who hold it for the good of others, and those who possess it simply for their personal advantage. In the former class one would put missionary priests, ship chaplains and chaplains of the armed forces. These priests enjoy the privilege of the portable altar chiefly for the spiritual benefit of those whom they serve. In the latter class one would place those priests who, by membership in various organizations within the Church, enjoy the privilege of using a portable altar while on vacation or while convalescing from an illness. One would also associate with these such laymen who have received this favor from the Holy See in recompense for some signal service to the Church.

On the basis of this division it can be argued that, since in the former case the welfare of those who attend the Mass is the reason for the granting of the privilege, they surely can fulfill the precept of hearing Mass. This situation is analogous to the one in which the bishop uses his *per modum actus* power of allowing Mass to be said outside a parish church. As long as there is not granted any dispensation from the law in its demand of the proper place for the fulfillment of the Sunday precept, the privilege is rendered nugatory in both of the cases here considered.

However, when the priest enjoys a purely personal privilege, so Regatillo argues, then only the person who enjoys the privilege, the celebrant and the minister, fulfill the Sunday precept. Since in most of the cases the recipient of the privilege is a priest, he and the server will be the only two who fulfill their obligation.[37]

The argument in support of this contention can still better be illustrated when the point in question is considered in connection with or in relation to a domestic oratory. Authorities both old and new are in agreement that the priest who says Mass in a private or domestic oratory thereby satisfies the Sunday precept as it applies to him. Ferraris (+ ca. 1763) argued that the decree of Clement XI, *Quoniam sancta,* given on December 15, 1703, barred from

[36] Regatillo, *op. cit.*, I, n. 223.

[37] Regatillo, *Ius Sacramentarium,* I, n. 223.

the possibility of fulfilling the precept only those who *hear* such a Mass. Neither the priest nor the server can be classed among the *audientes.*[38]

Gattico (1704–1754) likewise supported this interpretation, but with a reservation. He granted that the server could fulfill the precept only in the case that the person who enjoyed the privilege was not able or not willing to serve Mass himself.[39]

Among the authors who since the enactment of the present Code have expressed the doctrine of Gattico one may point to Coronata.[40] Other authors in their reference to the Code have advanced the same argument that Ferraris marshalled with reference to the decree of Pope Clement XI. Canon 1249 deals simply with the places where the law of *hearing* Mass may be fulfilled, and neither the priest nor the minister is to be classed as *audiens Missam.*[41]

Though this argument is advanced by the authors in their treatment of the question of private oratories, it is clearly applicable, with equal force, to the question of the privilege of the portable altar. It is equally true that the celebrant of Mass on a portable altar and the one who serves the Mass cannot be properly classed simply among the *audientes.* It can be safely concluded, then, that the celebrant who offers Mass on a portable altar in virtue of any kind of privilege or title that warrants his use of a portable altar fulfills thereby his Sunday or holy day obligation. It can also be maintained that the server of any Mass said in virtue of the privilege of the portable altar likewise fulfills his obligation of hearing Mass. Both of these statements have effect even when the privilege involved is a purely personal one; *a fortiori* they maintain their force when Mass is said in virtue of any other more extensive privilege. This opinion seems to have been sanctioned in a recent Instruction of the Sacred Congregation of the Sacraments[42] which quotes Gattico[43] to the effect that persons

[38] Ferraris, s. v. *Oratorium,* n. 5.

[39] Gattico, cap. XXV, n. 23.

[40] Coronata, *De Locis et Temporibus Sacris,* p. 93.

[41] Many, *De Locis Sacris,* n. 90; Vermeersch-Creusen, *Epitome Iuris Canonici,* II, n. 502; Guiniven, *The Precept of Hearing Mass,* p. 115.

[42] S. C. de Sacramentis, instr. *Quam plurimum,* 1 oct. 1949, II, 8—*AAS,* XLI (1949), 504.

[43] *De Oratoriis Domesticis et de Usu Altaris Portatilis,* cap. XV, n. 14.

other than those directly privileged can fulfill the Sunday precept only if the indult expressly says so. By inference then, those who are the direct recipients of the privilege can fulfill the obligation of a preceptive Mass by using the privilege even though nothing on that point is mentioned in the indult. This is also the conclusion drawn by Donnelly from his study of the text of the Instruction.[44]

The second point that must be discussed with reference to the privilege of the portable altar and the precept of hearing Mass is whether or not there exists an obligation to attend a Mass which is offered on a portable altar when that is the only means available for satisfying a preceptive Mass. If in a given case it is only possible to attend Mass which is said on a portable altar, is there an obligation to do so in fulfillment of the Sunday precept?

To discuss the particular cases in the relative order of their practical importance one should begin with the Mass that is said outside of a church when through a specific grant the bishop has utilized his *per modum actus* power as vindicated for him in canon 822, § 4. As has already been demonstrated, his canon paves the way for an implicit dispensation from the law of the proper place for the hearing of Mass. Attendance at Mass said under these conditions suffices for the fulfillment of the precept for the very reason that the Mass is being said precisely that that end might be served. It seems to follow logically that the faithful are under the obligation to attend this Mass and fulfill thereby the Sunday precept. When such extraordinary steps are taken for their accommodation, it would be very incongruous to bespeak for them an option which would leave them as free to remain away as it leaves them free also to attend.[45]

---

[44] Donnelly, "Indults for Portable Altar and Mass Without Server," *The Homiletic and Pastoral Review,* L (1950), 364.

[45] Vermeersch, "Dubia quaedam de ritibus missae, de praecepto audiendi missam, de praesentia in ordinatione," *Periodica,* XVI (1927), pp. 271* ff. Cf. Anonymous, "Satisfying the Obligation of Sunday Mass celebrated at a Portable Altar," *The Ecclesiastical Review* (from 1889–1905, and again from 1944, *The American Eccleciastical Review,* Philadelphia, 1889–1943; Baltimore, 1944–), C (1939), 69–70 (hereafter cited *ER* and *AER* respectively); Anonymous, "Assistance at Sunday Mass at Summer Camps," *ER,* C (1939), 71–72.

Among the ones for whom the foregoing has application there certainly should be listed the men in the armed forces for whom the service of chaplains is provided. While it is very true that no one can point to the letter of the law that binds them to attend Mass when it is said under circumstances not contemplated under canon 1249, yet the precarious mode of a soldier's existence, with its dreadful dangers besetting both body and soul, seems to accentuate his obligations which derive from the natural law itself, namely, not only to worship God but also to use the means at his disposal to safeguard his spiritual welfare. To this end chaplains possess almost unlimited faculties to dispense from ecclesiastical laws whenever the good of souls can thus be furthered. To say in the light of all this that the men thus served are under no obligation to attend Mass when it is said on a portable altar would be, in effect, to doubt the wisdom of the Church.

On the question of Mass at sea it has been reported as the teaching of authors that the obligation of hearing Mass can be fulfilled not only if the ship has its own oratory or when the Mass is said "*sub dio,*" but also if the Mass is said in any accessible place on the ship. Jombart made a study of the opinions on whether or not there is an obligation to attend Mass celebrated on board ship in an accessible place, for this point is not covered by the ruling which is contained in canon 1249.[46] He concluded that, while it is very probable that the precept of hearing Mass can be fulfilled under these circumstances, this probability, in itself, does not furnish a sufficient basis for urging an obligation upon the faithful to attend such a Mass when no other attendance at Mass is possible for them.

The various limitations with which the cited authors hedged their statements were deemed by Jombart as sufficient evidence that the alleged obligation could not be considered as binding with certainty. Gury (1801–1866)-Ferreres (1861–1936), for example, held that the seafarers aren't bound to attend a Mass which in virtue of a purely personal privilege is said by a priest in an accessible place.[47]

---

[46] Jombart, "De obligatione audiendi missam in mari," *Periodica,* XIX (1930), 124*–126*.

[47] Gury-Ferreres, *Compendium Theologiae Moralis* (editio tertia Hispana,

Vermeersch disagreed with the findings of Jombart by contending that when Mass is said on board ship in an accessible place the sea travelers are obliged to attend that Mass in order to fulfill the precept. He based this assertion both on the fact that the Index to the Code reveals that the obligation to hear Mass can be fulfilled anywhere but in a private oratory,[48] and also on the general obligation of sanctifying the Sabbath, which obligation is incumbent on all Catholics everywhere.[49]

Against the argument that is derived from the statement made in the Index of the Code, it can be said that the Index does not have the force of law, and moreover that in this case the wording of the Index is almost completely different from that of the canon to which it refers, namely canon 1249. It is readily conceivable that the wording of the Index simply indicates that attendance at Mass in one's own parish church is not necessary for the fulfillment of the precept.

While it is true that all people are enjoined to "keep holy the Sabbath day," the obligation to do so by attending Sunday Mass is of ecclesiastical rather than divine origin. It needs therefore to be fulfilled simply according to the conditions set down in the Church's law. These conditions are probably not met when Mass is said on board ship but simply in an accessible place. Hence the obligation cannot be urged.

Even conceding to the argument of Vermeersch whatever cogency it may possess, one does not thereby overthrow the fact that there is here a real doubt and controversy among the authors, as Jombart has shown. Consequently no obligation can be imposed on travelers at sea to attend a Mass said on board ship in an accessible place by a priest who possesses simply a personal privilege of the portable altar. The question of scandal or other factors may enter in to alter the situation, but fundamentally no

---

2 vols., Barcinone: Subirana Fratres, 1906), I, n. 348. Cf. Ubach, *Theologia Moralis Codici Juris Canonici accomodata* (2. ed., 2 vols., Bonis Auris: Sociedad San Miguel. 1935), I, n. 358.

[48] Cf. *Index analytico-alphabeticus Codicis Iuris Canonici s. v. Missa:* auditio: ". . . cui praecepto satisfaciunt Missam audiendo quocumque ritu ea celebratur et *ubivis,* exceptis oratoriis privatis . . ."

[49] Vermeersch, "Nota," *Periodica,* XIX (1930), 126*.

obligation can be urged. If the Mass is said in the ship's oratory or "*sub dio*," or in an accessible place *by the ship's chaplain*, then there is an obligation to attend the Mass; otherwise, there is not.

Moreover, in the circumstances in which there is no obligation on the part of the faithful to attend the Mass, there can be no strict obligation on the part of the priest to say the Mass for their benefit. In the case presented above, namely, that of Mass said in an accessible place on shipboard by a priest enjoying a purely personal privilege, since it is probable that the faithful cannot fulfill the precept, the priest cannot be strictly urged to say a Mass in order that a probably non-existent precept might be fulfilled.[50] The likelihood of resulting scandal if he did not say Mass for the people would, of course, make it incumbent upon the priest to use his privilege for their benefit. It will be seen in the subsequent section of this chapter that there exists a controversy among theologians on the question of whether or not a person is obliged to use a privilege in order to fulfill an obligation that arises purely from ecclesiastical law. There is no doubt, however, that if an obligation arises from the natural law, a person must avail himself of his privilege if the use of it provides the only means for satisfying the obligation. Since the obligation to avoid scandal arises from the natural law, there is no doubt that a priest would be bound to say Mass under the circumstances given above in order to avoid giving scandal.

Consequent to the discussion of the obligation of the faithful to attend Mass when it is said on a portable altar is the determining of the priest's obligation to say such a Mass in order to fulfill the Sunday precept as it applies to him. The solution of that question rests on the more fundamental problem of whether or not a priest is bound to use a privilege when the use of it presents the only means for the fulfillment of a precept of ecclesiastical law, or more precisely here, whether or not he is bound to use his privilege of the portable altar when otherwise he could not fulfill his Sunday precept.

Canon 69 states that no one is obliged to use a privilege that has

---

[50] Cf. Guiniven, *The Precept of Hearing Mass*, p. 116.

been granted in his own favor alone, unless an obligation to do so arises from some other source.[51]

Cicognani [52] in his commentary on this canon said that the word "*dumtaxat*" implies that a private grantee is obliged to use a privilege which was shared with him for the benefit of a group, in favor of a community, etc. He stressed the fact that the canon subjoins the qualification: "unless the obligation to use a privilege arises from some other source." If a moral bond arises from some other source, namely, from a law of the Church, and the obligation of this law can be fulfilled through a use of the privilege, then we are bound to use our privilege for the reason that we are held to fulfill the law, but can do so only by using our privilege. He gave the example of a sick priest who enjoys the privilege of a private oratory. If he cannot leave the house, he must say Mass in his private oratory if there is no great inconvenience involved. In place of the privilege of a private oratory one could readily contemplate the privilege of a portable altar without doing any violence to the logic of the example.

Roelker [53] likewise maintained that a privileged person is obliged to use his privilege in order that he may fulfill the law of the Church. "Generally speaking," he said, "the same obligation arises to use a privilege whenever by means of a privilege an obstacle is removed permitting the fulfillment of law or precept." He gave the same example of the sick priest enjoying the privilege of the private oratory and, after answering objections, concluded that the obligation of the Sunday precept seems to cancel the option that would attend the use of the privilege.

Guiniven,[54] upon citing other authorities, adopted this same view,

---

[51] Can. 69: "Nemo cogitur uti privilegio in sui dumtaxat favorem concesso, nisi alio ex capite exsurgat obligatio."

[52] *Canon Law* (authorized English version by J. M. O'Hara-F. Brennan, Philadelphia: Dolphin Press, 1934), p. 807.

[53] *Principles of Privilege according to the Code of Canon Law* (The Catholic University of America Canon Law Studies, n. 35, Washington, D. C.: The Catholic University of America, 1926), pp. 94, 95, footnote n. 28.

[54] *Precept of Hearing Mass,* pp. 147–148. Cf. Maroto, *Institutiones Iuris Canonici ad Normam Novi Codicis* (2 vols., Vol. I, 3. ed., Romae, 1921), I, n. 300, A, b; Marc-Gestermann, *Institutiones Morales Alphonsianae* (17. ed., 2 vols., Lugduni: Emmanuel Vitte, 1922), I, n. 251.

namely that if a person who enjoys a privilege cannot fulfill the precept of hearing Mass in any other way, he must make use of the privilege in order to fulfill the obligation.

More recently Furlong [55] has made a detailed study of this moral question and its development by theologians from the time of Suarez. Making mention of this same example, he concluded with Suarez and the majority of the authors he consulted that, when a privilege makes possible the observance of a law or a precept binding from another source, that privilege must be used.[56] Moreover, in answer to the objection that the obligatory use of a purely personal privilege is contrary to the Rule of Law, "quod ob gratiam alicuius conceditur non est in eius dispendium retorquendum," [57] he contended that the emerging obligation arises quite incidentally. " In ninety-nine cases out of one hundred," so he continued, " the privilege is entirely favorable. In setting up an objective norm of conduct for the privileged person differing in some respect from the general law, the Lawgiver cannot provide for exceptional cases." In the clause, " nisi alio ex capite exsurgat obligatio," as incorporated in canon 69, he sees the adaptation which the law invokes for the rarely occurring exceptional cases.[58]

While the present writer agrees with the foregoing opinion on its intrinsic merits, he yet feels that the weight of the opposition is sufficient to render the obligation doubtful. In this opposite stand Noldin-Schmitt, for example, alluded to the very same example of the priest who possesses the privilege of a private oratory.[59] They argued, as did Woywod (1880–1941),[60] that the privilege would indeed be of a strange character if it bound one to do things that one would not otherwise have to perform. Woywod claimed that it was the common opinion that no one is bound to use a privilege in order to fulfill an *ecclesiastical* law which

---

[55] *Moral Obligation in the Use of Privilege* (Rome, Pontificia Universitas Gregoriana, 1947), pp. 73–81.

[56] Furlong, *op. cit.*, p. 79.

[57] Reg. 61, R. J., in VI°.

[58] Furlong, *op. cit.*, pp. 80, 81.

[59] Noldin-Schmitt, *Summa Theologiae Moralis* (3 vols., Vol. I: *De Principiis,* 27. ed., Oeniponte/Lipsiae: Rauch, 1940), I, n. 195.

[60] *Commentary on the New Code of Canon Law,* I, n. 51.

without the use of the privilege one could not fulfill. Genicot-Salsmans and Coronata are likewise of this opinion.[61]

In view of this fundamental divergence of opinion among leading authors, it seems that no one can urge a grave obligation upon a priest to use his privilege of a portable altar in order to fulfill his obligation under the Sunday precept. The writer has endeavored to show that the celebrant and the server of a Mass, when it is said anywhere by virtue of the privilege of the portable altar, can by means of it fulfill the obligation of the Sunday precept, and also that it is the more probable opinion that they must do so. Moreover, if in composing his own conscience in this matter a man is convinced by the arguments which assert the existence of an obligation, then surely, if he totally abstracts from the principles of probabilism, it becomes necessary for him to use the privilege of the portable altar when his so doing furnishes the only means available for fulfilling the Sunday precept.

However in view of the principles of probabilism,[62] inasmuch as the opinion which favors one's freedom from this obligation is a solidly probable doctrine, no one, no matter what his personal convictions in the matter may be, can urge the obligation upon any priest to use his personal privilege of the portable altar even as the sole and exclusive means for his fulfillment of the Sunday precept.[63]

---

[61] Genicot-Salsmans, *Institutiones theologiae moralis,* I, n. 342; Coronata, *De Locis et Temporibus Sacris,* n. 292. Cf. Furlong, *Moral Obligation in the Use of Privilege,* p. 79.

[62] Cf. Davis, *Moral and Pastoral Theology* (4. ed., 4 vols., London: Sheed and Ward, 1943), I, 91 ff.

[63] Cf. Furlong, *Moral Obligation in the Use of Privilege,* p. 81.

CONCLUSIONS

The following conclusions are offered, either as revealing a new application of principles inherent in the law, or as evincing with stronger arguments and juridical support the claims of certain recognized and established probable opinions:

1. The open air and the underground are no longer to be considered as in themselves unsuitable locations for the celebration of the Sacrifice of the Mass. pp. 57, 58, 60.

2. The expression "*sub dio*" of canon 1249 is not to be construed as meaning "everywhere." pp. 58, 59.

3. The privilege of the portable altar as described in canon 822, § 3, excludes the celebrating of Mass in a bedroom. pp. 60, 61.

4. The use of the portable altar for Mass in an airplane is forbidden. p. 62.

5. The prohibition of the use of the privilege of the portable altar at sea applies also during voyages over lakes and rivers. pp. 63, 64.

6. If a ship has its own oratory, any priest may use the oratory to say Mass without obtaining a special indult for the celebration of Mass at sea, and also any priest who enjoys the privilege of the portable altar may say Mass in his own stateroom even though he has not obtained an indult for the celebration of Mass at sea. pp. 64–67.

7. The need which exists for a group of the faithful to fulfill the Sunday precept is not the sole cause for which the ordinary can use the power granted to him by canon 822, § 4. pp. 73–75.

8. The extraordinary nature of the case in canon 822, § 4, need only be such in relation to the universal Church; and the permission which is granted "*per modum actus*" can safely be interpreted as allowing the celebration of several Masses in virtue of a single granted permission. pp. 75–79.

9. Within the strict letter of the law an ordinary can delegate the faculty which he possesses in virtue of canon 822, § 4, to

some priest, who can then use this power *per modum actus* repeatedly. pp. 69, 79.

10. All religious in general enjoy the privilege of the portable altar at least while they are engaged in mission work. pp. 88–90.

11. Priest members of Third Orders Secular of religious institutes which enjoy the privilege of the portable altar do not through their membership share in the same privilege. p. 90.

12. Priests who became perpetual members of the Missionary Union of the Clergy before August 1941 continue to enjoy the privilege of the portable altar for their use while on vacation. pp. 90–93.

13. Attendance at Mass which is said on a portable altar in consequence of an ordinary's utilization of the faculty which canon 822, § 4, accords to him suffices for satisfying the precept of hearing Mass, and those for whose benefit the granted power is used are obliged to attend that Mass if they cannot fulfill the precept in any other way. pp. 97–100, 108–109.

14. A Mass said contrary to the prescriptions of canon 822, § 4, does not provide a means for fulfilling the obligation to hear Mass. pp. 104–105.

15. The use of a purely personal privilege of the portable altar does not provide a means whereby the faithful may fulfill the obligation of a preceptive Mass. pp. 99–102.

16. The celebrant and the server of a Mass which is said on a portable altar anywhere can by means of it fulfill the obligation of the Sunday precept. pp. 106–107.

17. When Mass is said on a portable altar by virtue of a privilege that is not merely and purely personal, then those who are to derive the benefit from the utilized privilege may fulfill the obligation of hearing Mass. pp. 105–106, 97–99.

18. It seems the more probable opinion that one must use the granted privilege of the portable altar if otherwise one remained without a means for fulfilling the Sunday precept. pp. 111–115.

BIBLIOGRAPHY

SOURCES

Acta Apostolicae Sedis, Commentarium Officiale, Romae, 1909– .

Bullarium Franciscanum, 4 vols., Romae, 1759–1768.

Bullarium Ordinis Praedicatorum, 8 vols., Romae, 1729–1740.

Bullarum Diplomatum et Privilegiorum Sanctorum Romanorum Pontificum Taurinensis Editio, 24 vols., et Appendix Augustae Taurinorum, Neapoli, 1857–1872.

Codex Iuris Canonici Pii X Pontificis Maximi iussu digestus Benedictae Papae auctoritate promulgatus, Romae: Typis Polyglottis Vaticanis, 1917.

Codicis Iuris Canonici Fontes, cura Emi Petri Card. Gasparri editi, 9 vols., Romae (postea Civitate Vaticana): Typis Polyglottis Vaticanis, 1923–1939. (Vols. VII–IX, ed. cura et studio Emi Iustiniani Card. Serédi.

Collectanea S. Congregationis de Propaganda Fide, Romae: Typographia Polyglotta S. C. de Propaganda Fide, 1893.

Concilium Tridentinum, Diariorum, Actorum, Epistularum, Tractatuum, Nova Collectio. Edidit Societas Goerresiana. 13 vols., Friburgi Brisgoviae: B. Herder. 1901–1938.

Corpus Iuris Canonici, ed. Lipsien. 2., post Aemilii Ludovici Richteri curas instruxit Aemilius Friedberg, 2 vols., Lipsiae: Ex Officina Bernhardi Tauchnitz, 1879–1881. Editio anastatice repetita, Lipsiae: Tauchnitz, 1922.

Decreta Authentica Congregationis Sacrorum Rituum, 6 vols., Romae: Ex Typographis Polyglotta, 1898–1927.

Decretales D. Gregorii Papae IX suae integritate una cum glossis restitutae, cum privilegio Gregorii XIII, Pont. Max., et aliorum Principum, Romae, 1582.

Decretum Gratiani emendatum et notationibus illustratum una cum glossis, Gregorii XIII, Pont. Max., iussu editum, 2 vols., Romae, 1582.

Facultates Castrenses ad Usum Cappellanorum Copiis Armatis Statuum Foederatorum Americae Septentrionalis Addictorum, editio tertia, 1948.

Hardouin, Jean, *Acta Conciliorum et Epistolae Decretales ac Constitutiones Summorum Pontificum,* 12 vols., Parisiis, 1714–1715.

Liber Sextus Decretalium D. Bonifacii Papae VIII suae integretati una cum Clementinis et Extravagantibus earumque Glossis restitutis, Romae, 1582.

Mansi, Ioannes, *Sacrorum Conciliorum Nova et Amplissima Collectio,* 53 vols. in 60, Parisiis, 1901–1927.

Monumenta Germaniae Historica, 188 vols. incomplete, Hannoverae, 1826–. *Leges in 4,* Sectio II (*Capitularia Regum Francorum*), T. I, ed. A. Boretius, 1883; Sectio III (*Concilia*), T. II, ed. A. Werminghoff, 1906–1908.

Monumentorum ad Historiam Concilii Tridentini Collectio, 6 vols., Lovanii, 1785.

Pii IX Pontificis Maximi Acta, 9 vols., Romae: Ex Typographia Bonorum Artium, 1854–1878.

Potthast, A., *Regesta Pontificum Romanorum inde ab anno post Christum natum MCXCVIII ad annum MCCCIV,* 2 vols., Berolini, 1874–1875.

REFERENCE WORKS

Alphonsus M. de Liguori, St., *Theologia Moralis,* ed. L. Gaudé, 4 vols., Romae, 1905–1912.

Amort, Eus., *Elementa Juris Canonici Veteris et Moderni,* 3 vols., Ferrariae, 1763.

Aquinas, S. Thomas, *Summa Theologica,* ed. Marietti, 6 vols., Taurini Romae: Marietti, 1937.

Augustine, Charles, *A Commentary on the New Code of Canon Law,* 2. ed., 8 vols., St. Louis, Mo.: Herder & Co., 1918–1924.

Barbosa, Augustinus, *Iuris Ecclesiastici Universi Libri Tres,* 3 vols. in 2, Lugduni, 1660.

Beda Venerabilis, *Opera Quae Supersunt Omnia,* edidit J. A. Giles, 12 vols., Londini, 1843–1844.

Benedictus XIV, *De Sacrosancto Missae Sacrificio,* 3 vols., Prati, 1843.

Benko, Matthew, *The Abbot* NULLIUS, The Catholic University of America Canon Law Studies, n. 173, Washington, D. C.: The Catholic University of America Press, 1943.

Beste, U., *Introductio in Codicem,* 3. ed., Collegeville, Minn.: St. John's Abbey Press, 1946.

Blat, Albertus, *Commentarium Textus Codicis Iuris Canonici,* 5 vols. in 7, Vol. III, pars I (*De Sacramentis*), Romae: Ex Typographia Pontificia in Instituto Pii X, 1924.

Bliley, Nicholas, *Altars According to the Code of Canon Law,* The Catholic University of America Canon Law Studies, n. 38, Washington, D. C.: The Catholic University of America, 1927.

Bona, Ioannes, *Rerum Liturgicarum Libri Duo,* Romae, 1671.

Bouscaren, T. Lincoln, *The Canon Law Digest,* 2 vols., Milwaukee, Wis.: The Bruce Publishing Co., 1934–1943.

Bouscaren, T. L.-Ellis, Adam, *Canon Law,* Milwaukee, Wis.: The Bruce Publishing Co., 1946.

Braun, C., *Der christliche Altar in seiner geschichtlichen Entwicklung,* 2 vols., Muenchen: Alte Meister Guenther Koch & Co., 1924.

Cappello, F., *Tractatus Canonico-Moralis de Sacramentis;* 3 vols. in 6, Vol. I, 4. ed., Romae: Domus Editoralis Marietti, 1945.

Catholic Encyclopedia, The, 15 vols., Index and 2 supplements, New York, 1907–1922.

Cicognani, Amleto, *Canon Law,* authorized English version by J. M. O'Hara and F. Brennan, Philadelphia: Dolphin Press, 1934.

Coronata, Matthaeus Conte a, *De Locis et Temporibus Sacris,* Augustae Taurinorum: Marietti, 1922.

———, *Institutiones Iuris Canonici,* 2. ed., 5 vols., Taurini: Marietti, 1939–1947.

Davis, Henry, *Moral and Pastoral Theology,* 4. ed., 4 vols., London: Sheed and Ward, 1943.

De Lugo, I., *Disputationes Scholasticae et Morales,* 8 vols., Parisiis, 1868–1869.

De Meester, A., *Juris Canonici et Juris Canonico-Civilis Compendium,* nova editio, 3 vols. in 4, Brugis: Desclée de Brouwer et Soc., 1921–1928.

Fagnanus, Prosper, *Commentaria in Quinque Libros Decretalium,* 5 vols. in 3, Venetiis, 1696.

Ferraris, Lucius, *Bibliotheca Canonica, Iuridica, Moralis, Theologica, necnon Ascetica, Polemica, Rubristica, Historica, ed. noviss.,* 9 vols., Romae, 1885–1899.

Furlong, Francis, *Moral Obligation in the Use of Privilege,* Rome: Pontificia Universitas Gregoriana, 1947.

Gasparri, Petrus, *Tractatus Canonicus de Sanctissima Eucharistia,* 2 vols., Parisiis, 1897.

Gattico, Ioannes, *De Oratoriis Domesticis et de Usu Altaris Portatilis,* Romae, 1746.

Genicot, E.-Salsmans, I., *Institutiones Theologiae Moralis,* 13. ed., 2 vols., Bruxelles: Edition Universelle, 1936.

Guiniven, John, *The Precept of Hearing Mass,* The Catholic University of America Canon Law Studies, n. 158, Washington, D. C.: The Catholic University of America Press, 1942.

Gury, Ioannes-Ferreres, Ioannes, *Compendium Theologiae Moralis,* editio tertia Hispana, 2 vols., Barcinone: Subirana Fratres, 1906.

Henny, Hans, *Der Altar im kanonischen Recht,* Romae: Pontificia Universitas Gregoriana, 1940.

Hostiensis, Cardinalis (Henricus de Segusio), *Commentaria in Quinque Libros Decretalium,* 5 vols., Venetiis, 1581.

Hynes, Harry Gerard, *The Privileges of Cardinals,* The Catholic University of America Canon Law Studies, n. 217, Washington, D. C.: The Catholic University of America Press, 1945.

Lehmkuhl, Augustinus, *Theologia Moralis,* 9. ed., 2 vols., Friburgi Brisgoviae: Herder, 1898.

McDonough, Thomas, *Apostolic Administrators,* The Catholic University of America Canon Law Studies, n. 139, Washington, D. C.: The Catholic University of America Press, 1941.

Mabillon, I., *Acta Sanctorum Ordinis Sancti Benedicti,* 6 vols. in 9, Venetiis, 1733.

Many, S., *Praelectiones Canonicae de Locis Sacris,* Parisiis, 1904.

———, *Praelectiones de Missa,* Parisiis, 1903.

Marc, Clemens-Gestermann, Fr. X., *Institutiones Morales Alphonsianae,* 17. ed., 2 vols., Lugduni: Emmanuel Vitte, 1922.

Maroto, Philippus, *Institutiones Iuris Canonici ad Normam Novi Codicis,* 2 vols., Vol. I, 3. ed., Romae, 1921.

Martène, E., *De Antiquis Ecclesiae Ritibus,* 3 vols., Rotomagi, 1700–1702.

Matulenas, Raymond, *Communication, A Source of Privileges,* The Catholic University of America Canon Law Studies, n. 183, Washington, D. C.: The Catholic University of America Press, 1943.

Migne, J. P., *Patrologiae Cursus Completus, Series Latina,* 221 vols., Parisiis, 1844–1864.

———, *Series Graeca,* 161 vols., Parisiis, 1857–1866.

Noldin, H.-Schmitt, A., *Summa Theologia Moralis,* 3 vols., Vol. I (*De Principiis*), 27. ed., Oeniponte/Lipsiae: Rauch, 1940.

Ojetti, B., *Synopsis Rerum Moralium et Iuris Pontificii alphabetico ordine digesta,* 3. ed., 4 vols., Romae, 1909–1914.

Panormitanus, Abbas (Nicholaus de Tudeschis), *Commentaria in Quinque Libros Decretalium,* 5 vols. in 7, Venetiis, 1588.

Petra, V., *Commentaria ad Constitutiones Apostolicas,* 5 vols. in 2, Venetiis, 1729.

Prümmer, Dominicus, *Manuale Theologiae Moralis,* 5. ed., 8 vols., Friburgi Brisgoviae: Herder & Co., 1928.

Raymundus de Peñaforte, *Summa,* nova editio, Veronae, 1744.

Regatillo, E., *Ius Sacramentarium,* 2 vols., Santander: Sal Terrae, 1945–1946.

Reiffenstuel, Anacletus, *Jus Canonicum Universum,* 5 vols. in 7, Parisiis, 1864–1870.

Roelker, Edward, *Principles of Privilege according to the Code of Canon Law,* The Catholic University of America Canon Law Studies, n. 35, Washington, D. C.: The Catholic University of America, 1926.

Snee, Joseph-Clark, J. Donald, *Diocesan Faculties in the United States,* Woodstock, Md.: Woodstock College Press, 1948.

Suarez, Franciscus, *Opera Omnia,* editio nova, 26 vols. et Index, Parisiis, 1856–1878.

Thalhofer, F. H., *Handbuch der katholischen Liturgik,* 1. ed., 2 vols., Freiburg im Breisgau, 1883–1893; 2. ed., a L. Eisenhofer, 2 vols., Freiburg im Breisgau, 1912.

Thiers, Jean Baptiste, *Dissertation ecclésiastique sur les principeaux autels des églises, les jubés des églises, la clôture des choeurs des églises,* Paris, 1688.

Thomassin, Louis, *Vetus et Nova Ecclesiae Disciplina circa Beneficia et Beneficiarios,* 10 vols., Magontiaci, 1787.

Ubach, I., *Theologia Moralis Codici Iuris Canonici accomodata,* 2. ed., 2 vols., Buenos-Aires: Sociedad San Miguel, 1935.

Van-Espen, Zegerus, *Jus Ecclesiasticum Universum,* 4 vols., Lovanii, 1778.

Van Hove, A., *Tractatus de Sanctissima Eucharistia,* 2. ed., Mechliniae: Dessain, 1941.

Vermeersch, Arturus-Creusen, Josephus, *Epitome Iuris Canonici,* 6. ed., 3 vols., Mechliniae-Romae: Dessain, 1937–1946.

Wernz, F. X., *Ius Decretalium,* 3. ed., 6 vols., Prati, 1913–1915.

Wernz, F. X.-Vidal, P., *Ius Canonicum,* 7 vols. in 8, Tom. II (*De Personis*), 3. ed., 1943, Romae: Apud Aedes Universitatis Gregorianae; Tom. IV, Vol. I, 1934.

Woywod, Stanislaus, *A Practical Commentary on the Code of Canon Law,* 10. printing, 2 vols., New York: Joseph F. Wagner, 1946.

ARTICLES

Anonymous, "Assistance at Sunday Mass at Summer Camps," *ER,* C (1939), 71–72.

———, "Satisfying the Obligation of Sunday Mass Celebrated at a Portable Altar," *ER,* C (1939), 69–70.

Bastnagel, Clement, "Cases and Studies," *The Jurist,* II (1942), 155–158.

Bouscaren, T. Lincoln, "De Missa ex licentia Ordinarii celebrata," *Periodica,* XXVIII (1939), 52–61.

Donnelly, Francis B., "Indults for Portable Altar and Mass Without Server," *The Homiletic and Pastoral Review,* L (1950), 363–364.

Goyenche, S., "Commentarium in Responsum ad Can. 613, § 1," *Apollinaris,* XI (1938), 178–180.

Hannan, Jerome, "Holy Mass Aboard Ship," *The Jurist,* VIII (1949), 70–71.

Jombart, E., "De obligatione audiendi Missam in mari," *Periodica,* XIX (1930), 124*–126*.

Vermeersch, A., "Nota," *Periodica,* XIX (1930), 126*–127*.

———, "Dubie quaedam de ritibus missae, de praecepto audiendi missam, de praesentia in ordinatione," *Periodica,* XVI (1927), 266*–279*.

PERIODICALS

American Ecclesiastical Review, The, Vols. I–XXXII, Philadelphia, 1889–1905; from 1905: *The Ecclesiastical Review,* Vols. XXXIII–CIX, Philadelphia, 1905–1943; from 1944: *The American Ecclesiastical Review,* Washington, D. C., Vol. CX, 1944– .

Apollinaris, Romae, 1928– .

Denver Register, The, Denver, Colo.

Homiletic and Pastoral Review, The, New York, 1900– .

Jurist, The, Washington, D. C., 1941– .

Periodica de Religiosis et Missionariis, Brugis, 1905–1919; *Periodica de Re Canonica et Morali Utili praesertim Religiosis et Missionariis,* Brugis, 1920–1927; *Periodica de Re Morali, Canonica, Liturgica,* Brugis, 1927–1936; Romae, 1937– .

ABBREVIATIONS

AAS—*Acta Apostolicae Sedis.*
AER—*The American Ecclesiastical Review.*
Bull. Rom.—*Bullarum Diplomatum et Privilegiorum Sanctorum Romanorum Pontificum Taurinensis Editio.*
Collectanea—*Collectanea S. Congregationis de Propaganda Fide.*
ER—*The Ecclesiastical Review.*
Fontes—*Codicis Iuris Canonici Fontes cura . . . Gasparri editi.*
Hardouin—*Acta Conciliorum et Epistolae Decretales ac Constitutiones Summorum Pontificum.*
Mansi—*Sacrorum Conciliorum Nova et Amplissima Collectio.*
MGH—*Monumenta Germaniae Historica.*
MPG—Migne, *Patrologia Graeca.*
MPL—Migne, *Patrologia Latina.*
P. C. I.—Pontificia Commissio Interpretationis.
Periodica—*Periodica de Re Morali, Canonica, Liturgica.*
S. C. C.—Sacra Congregatio Concilii.
S. C. Consist.—Sacra Congregatio Consistorialis.
S. C. de Prop. Fide—Sacra Congregatio de Propaganda Fide.
S. C. de Sacramentis—Sacra Congregatio de Sacramentis.
S. R. C.—Sacrorum Rituum Congregatio.

BIOGRAPHICAL NOTE

Thomas J. Welsh was born on December 20, 1921, in Weatherly, Pennsylvania. There he attended Saint Nicholas' Parochial School and Schwab High School. On September 1, 1937, he entered Saint Charles' Seminary, Overbrook, Pa., where he received the degree of Bachelor of Arts in 1943. He was ordained to the priesthood on May 30, 1946. The following October he entered the Catholic University of America to pursue graduate studies in the School of Canon Law. He received the Baccalaureate Degree in Canon Law in June, 1947, and the Licentiate Degree in Canon Law in June, 1948.

ALPHABETICAL INDEX

CANON LAW STUDIES *

1. FRERIKS, REV. CELESTINE A., C.PP.S., J.C.D., Religious Congregations in Their External Relations, 121 pp., 1916.
2. GALLIHER, REV. DANIEL M., O.P., J.C.D., Canonical Elections, 117 pp., 1917.
3. BORKOWSKI, REV. AURELIUS L., O.F.M., J.C.D., De Confraternitatibus Ecclesiasticis, 136 pp., 1918.
4. CASTILLO, REV. CAYO, J.C.D., Disertacion Historico-Canonica sobre la Potestad del Cabildo en Sede Vacante o Impedida del Vicario Capitular, 99 pp., 1919 (1918).
5. KUBELBECK, REV. WILLIAM J., S.T.B., J.C.D., The Sacred Penitentiaria and Its Relation to Faculties of Ordinaries and Priests, 129 pp., 1918.
6. PETROVITS, REV. JOSEPH J. C., S.T.D., J.C.D., The New Church Law on Matrimony, X-461 pp., 1919.
7. HICKEY, REV. JOHN J., S.T.B., J.C.D., Irregularities and Simple Impediments in the New Code of Canon Law, 100 pp., 1920.
8. KLEKOTKA, REV. PETER J., S.T.B., J.C.D., Diocesan Consultors, 179 pp., 1920.
9. WANENMACHER, REV. FRANCIS, J.C.D., The Evidence in Ecclesiastical Procedure Affecting the Marriage Bond, 1920 (Printed 1935).
10. GOLDEN, REV. HENRY FRANCIS, J.C.D., Parochial Benefices in the New Code, IV-119 pp., 1921 (Printed 1925).
11. KOUDELKA, REV. CHARLES J., J.C.D., Pastors, Their Rights and Duties According to the New Code of Canon Law, 211 pp., 1921.
12. MELO, REV. ANTONIUS, O.F.M., J.C.D., De Exemptione Regularium, X-188 pp., 1921.
13. SCHAAF, REV. VALENTINE THEODORE, O.F.M., S.T.B., J.C.D., The Cloister, X-180 pp., 1921.
14. BURKE, REV. THOMAS JOSEPH, S.T.D., J.C.D., Competence in Ecclesiastical Tribunals, IV-117 pp., 1922.
15. LEECH, REV. GEORGE LEO, J.C.D., A Comparative Study of the Constitution "Apostolicae Sedis" and the "Codex Juris Canonici," 179 pp., 1922.
16. MOTRY, REV. HUBERT LOUIS, S.T.D., J.C.D., Diocesan Faculties According to the Code of Canon Law, II-167 pp., 1922.
17. MURPHY, REV. GEORGE LAWRENCE, J.C.D., Delinquencies and Penalties in the Administration and the Reception of the Sacraments, IV-121 pp., 1923.

* All published numbers are available from the Catholic University of America Press, 621 Michigan Ave., N.E., Washington 17, D. C., except the following numbers: 1-114 inclusive, and numbers 116, 118, 120, 122, 123, 162 and 198.

18. O'Reilly, Rev. John Anthony, S.T.B., J.C.D., Ecclesiastical Sepulture in the New Code of Canon Law, II-129 pp., 1923.
19. Michalicka, Rev. Wenceslas Cyrill, O.S.B., J.C.D., Judicial Procedure in Dismissal of Clerical Exempt Religious, 107 pp., 1923.
20. Dargin, Rev. Edward Vincent, S.T.B., J.C.D., Reserved Cases According to the Code of Canon Law, IV-103 pp., 1924.
21. Godfrey, Rev. John A., S.T.B., J.C.D., The Right of Patronage According to the Code of Canon Law, 153 pp., 1924.
22. Hagedorn, Rev. Francis Edward, J.C.D., General Legislation on Indulgences, II-154 pp., 1924.
23. King, Rev. James Ignatius, J.C.D., The Administration of the Sacraments to Dying Non-Catholics, V-141 pp., 1924.
24. Winslow, Rev. Francis Joseph, M.M., J.C.D., Vicars and Prefects Apostolic, IV-149 pp., 1924.
25. Correa, Rev. Jose Servelion, S.T.L., J.C.D., La Potestad Legislativa de la Iglesia Catolica, IV-127 pp., 1925.
26. Dugan, Rev. Henry Francis, A.M., J.C.D., The Judiciary Department of the Diocesan Curia, 87 pp., 1925.
27. Keller, Rev. Charles Frederick, S.T.B., J.C.D., Mass Stipends, 167 pp., 1925.
28. Paschang, Rev. John Linus, J.C.D., The Sacramentals According to the Code of Canon Law, 129 pp., 1925.
29. Piontek, Rev. Cyrillus, O.F.M., S.T.B., J.C.D., De Indulto Exclaustrationis necnon Saecularizationis, XIII-289 pp., 1925.
30. Kearney, Rev. Richard Joseph, S.T.B., J.C.D., Sponsors at Baptism According to the Code of Canon Law, IV-127 pp., 1925.
31. Bartlett, Rev. Chester Joseph, A.M., LL.B., J.C.D., The Tenure of Parochial Property in the United States of America, V-108 pp., 1926.
32. Kilker, Rev. Adrian Jerome, J.C.D., Extreme Unction, V-425 pp., 1926.
33. McCormick, Rev. Robert Emmett, J.C.D., Confessors of Religious, VIII-266 pp., 1926.
34. Miller, Rev. Newton Thomas, J.C.D., Founded Masses According to the Code of Canon Law, VII-93 pp., 1926.
35. Roelker, Rev. Edward G., S.T.D., J.C.D., Principles of Privilege According to the Code of Canon Law, XI-166 pp., 1926.
36. Bakalarczyk, Rev. Richardus, M.I.C., J.U.D., De Novitiatu, VIII-208 pp., 1927.
37. Pizzuti, Rev. Lawrence, O.F.M., J.U.L., De Parochis Religiosis, 1927. (Not Printed.)
38. Bliley, Rev. Nicholas Martin, O.S.B., J.C.D., Altars According to the Code of Canon Law, XIX-132 pp., 1927.
39. Brown, Mr. Brendan Francis, A.B., LL.M., J.U.D., The Canonical Juristic Personality with Special Reference to its Status in the United States of America, V-212 pp., 1927.

40. Cavanaugh, Rev. William Thomas, C.P., J.U.D., The Reservation of the Blessed Sacrament, VIII-101 pp., 1927.
41. Doheny, Rev. William J., C.S.C., A.B., J.U.D., Church Property: Modes of Acquisition, X-118 pp., 1927.
42. Feldhaus, Rev. Aloysius H., C.PP.S., J.C.D., Oratories, IX-141 pp., 1927.
43. Kelly, Rev. James Patrick, A.B., J.C.D., The Jurisdiction of the Simple Confessor, X-208 pp., 1927.
44. Neuberger, Rev. Nicholas J., J.C.D., Canon 6 or the Relation of the Codex Juris Canonici to the Preceding Legislation, V-95 pp., 1927.
45. O'Keefe, Rev. Gerald Michael, J.C.D., Matrimonial Dispensations, Powers of Bishops, Priests, and Confessors, VIII-232 pp., 1927.
46. Quigley, Rev. Joseph A. M., A.B., J.C.D., Condemned Societies, 139 pp., 1927.
47. Zaplotnik, Rev. Johannes Leo, J.C.D., De Vicariis Foraneis, X-142 pp., 1927.
48. Duskie, Rev. John Aloysius, A.B., J.C.D., The Canonical Status of the Orientals in the United States, VIII-196 pp., 1928.
49. Hyland, Rev. Francis Edward, J.C.D., Excommunication, Its Nature, Historical Development and Effects, VIII-181 pp., 1928.
50. Reinmann, Rev. Gerald Joseph, O.M.C., J.C.D., The Third Order Secular of Saint Francis, 201 pp., 1928.
51. Schenk, Rev. Francis J., J.C.D., The Matrimonial Impediments of Mixed Religion and Disparity of Cult, XVI-318 pp., 1929.
52. Coady, Rev. John Joseph, S.T.D., J.U.D., A.M., The Appointment of Pastors, VIII-150 pp., 1929.
53. Kay, Rev. Thomas Henry, J.C.D., Competence in Matrimonial Procedure, VIII-164 pp., 1929.
54. Turner, Rev. Sidney Joseph, C.P., J.U.D., The Vow of Poverty, XLIX-217 pp., 1929.
55. Kearney, Rev. Raymond A., A.B., S.T.D., J.C.D., The Principles of Delegation, VII-149 pp., 1929.
56. Conran, Rev. Edward James, A.B., J.C.D., The Interdict, V-163 pp., 1930.
57. O'Neill, Rev. William H., J.C.D., Papal Rescripts of Favor, VII-218 pp., 1930.
58. Bastnagel, Rev. Clement Vincent, J.U.D., The Appointment of Parochial Adjutants and Assistants, XV-257 pp., 1930.
59. Ferry, Rev. William A., A.B., J.C.D., Stole Fees, V-136 pp., 1930.
60. Costello, Rev. John Michael, A.B., J.C.D., Domicile and Quasi-Domicile, VII-201 pp., 1930.
61. Kremer, Rev. Michael Nicholas, A.B., S.T.B., J.C.D., Church Support in the United States, VI-136 pp., 1930.
62. Angulo, Rev. Luis, C.M., J.C.D., Legislation de la Iglesia sobre la intencion en la application de la Santa Misa, VII-104 pp., 1931.

63. Frey, Rev. Wolfgang Norbert, O.S.B., A.B., J.C.D., The Act of Religious Profession, VIII-174 pp., 1931.
64. Roberts, Rev. James Brendan, A.B., J.C.D., The Banns of Marriage, XIV-140 pp., 1931.
65. Ryder, Rev. Raymond Aloysius, A.B., J.C.D., Simony, IX-151 pp., 1931.
66. Campagna, Rev. Angelo, Ph.D., J.U.D., Il Vicario Generale del Vescovo, VII-205 pp., 1931.
67. Cox, Rev. Joseph Godfrey, A.B., J.C.D., The Administration of Seminaries, VI-124 pp., 1931.
68. Gregory, Rev. Donald J., J.U.D., The Pauline Privilege, XV-165 pp., 1931.
69. Donohue, Rev. John F., J.C.D., The Impediment of Crime, VII-110 pp., 1931.
70. Dooley, Rev. Eugene A., O.M.I., J.C.D., Church Law on Sacred Relics, IX-143 pp., 1931.
71. Orth, Rev. Clement Raymond, O.M.C., J.C.D., The Approbation of Religious Institutes, 171 pp., 1931.
72. Pernicone, Rev. Joseph M., A.B., J.C.D., The Ecclesiastical Prohibition of Books, XII-267 pp., 1932.
73. Clinton, Rev. Connell, A.B., J.C.D., The Paschal Precept, IX-108 pp., 1932.
74. Donnelly, Rev. Francis B., A.M., S.T.L., J.C.D., The Diocesan Synod, VIII-125 pp., 1932.
75. Torrente, Rev. Camilo, C.M.F., J.C.D., Las Procesiones Sagradas, V-145 pp., 1932.
76. Murphy, Rev. Edwin J., C.PP.S., J.C.D., Suspension Ex Informata Conscientia, XI-122 pp., 1932.
77. MacKenzie, Rev. Eric F., A.M., S.T.L., J.C.D., The Delict of Heresy in its Commission, Penalization, Absolution, VII-124 pp., 1932.
78. Lyons, Rev. Avitus E., S.T.B., J.C.D., The Collegiate Tribunal of First Instance, XI-147 pp., 1932.
79. Connolly, Rev. Thomas A., J.C.D., Appeals, XI-195 pp., 1932.
80. Sangmeister, Rev. Joseph V., A.B., J.C.D., Force and Fear as Precluding Matrimonial Consent, V-211 pp., 1932.
81. Jaeger, Rev. Leo A., A.B., J.C.D., The Administration of Vacant and Quasi-Vacant Episcopal Sees in the United States, IX-229 pp., 1932.
82. Rimlinger, Rev. Herbert T., J.C.D., Error Invalidating Matrimonial Consent, VII-79 pp., 1932.
83. Barrett, Rev. John D. M., S.S., J.C.D., A Comparative Study of the Third Plenary Council of Baltimore and the Code, IX-221 pp., 1932.
84. Carberry, Rev. John J., Ph.D., S.T.D., J.C.D., The Juridical Form of Marriage, X-177 pp., 1934.
85. Dolan, Rev. John L., A.B., J.C.D., The Defensor Vinculi, XII-157 pp., 1934.

86. HANNAN, REV. JEROME D., A.M., S.T.D., LL.B., J.C.D., The Canon Law of Wills, IX-517 pp., 1934.
87. LEMIEUX, REV. DELISE A., A.M., J.C.D., The Sentence in Ecclesiastical Procedure, IX-131 pp., 1934.
88. O'ROURKE, REV. JAMES J., A.B., J.C.D., Parish Registers, VII-109 pp., 1934.
89. TIMLIN, REV. BARTHOLOMEW, O.F.M., A.M., J.C.D., Conditional Matrimonial Consent, X-381 pp., 1934.
90. WAHL, REV. FRANCIS X., A.B., J.C.D., The Matrimonial Impediments of Consanguinity and Affinity, VI-125 pp., 1934.
91. WHITE, REV. ROBERT J., A.B., LL.B., S.T.B., J.C.D., Canonical Ante-Nuptial Promises and the Civil Law, VI-152 pp., 1934.
92. HERRERA, REV. ANTONIO PARRA, O.C.D., J.C.D., Legislacion Ecclesiastica sobra el Ayuno y la Abstinencia, XI-191 pp., 1935.
93. KENNEDY, REV. EDWIN J., J.C.D., The Special Matrimonial Process in Cases of Evident Nullity, X-165 pp., 1935.
94. MANNING, REV. JOHN J., A.B., J.C.D., Presumption of Law in Matrimonial Procedure, XI-111 pp., 1935.
95. MOEDER, REV. JOHN M., J.C.D., The Proper Bishop for Ordination and Dimissorial Letters, VII-135 pp., 1935.
96. O'MARA, REV. WILLIAM A., A.B., J.C.D., Canonical Causes for Matrimonial Dispensations, IX-155 pp., 1935.
97. REILLY, REV. PETER, J.C.D., Residence of Pastors, IX-81 pp., 1935.
98. SMITH, REV. MARINER T., O.P., S.T.Lr., J.C.D., The Penal Law for Religious, VII-169 pp., 1935.
99. WHALEN, REV. DONALD W., A.M., J.C.D., The Value of Testimonial Evidence in Matrimonial Procedure, XIII-297 pp., 1935.
100. CLEARY, REV. JOSEPH F., J.C.D., Canonical Limitations on the Alienation of Church Property, VIII-141 pp., 1936.
101. GLYNN, REV. JOHN C., J.C.D., The Promoter of Justice, XX-337 pp., 1936.
102. BRENNAN, REV. JAMES H., S.S., M.A., S.T.B., J.C.D., The Simple Convalidation of Marriage, VI-135 pp., 1937.
103. BRUNINI, REV. JOSEPH BERNARD, J.C.D., The Clerical Obligations of Canons 139 and 142, X-121 pp., 1937.
104. CONNOR, REV. MAURICE, A.B., J.C.D., The Administrative Removal of Pastors, VIII-159 pp., 1937.
105. GUILFOYLE, REV. MERLIN JOSEPH, J.C.D., Custom, XI-144 pp., 1937.
106. HUGHES, REV. JAMES AUSTIN, A.B., A.M., J.C.D., Witnesses in Criminal Trials of Clerics, IX-140 pp., 1937.
107. JANSEN, REV. RAYMOND J., A.B., S.T.L., J.C.D., Canonical Provisions for Catechetical Instruction, VII-153 pp., 1937.
108. KEALY, REV. JOHN JAMES, A.B., J.C.D., The Introductory Libellus in Church Court Procedure, XI-121 pp., 1937.

109. McManus, Rev. James Edward, C.SS.R., J.C.D., The Administration of Temporal Goods in Religious Institutes, XVI-196 pp., 1937.
110. Moriarty, Rev. Eugene James, J.C.D., Oaths in Ecclesiastical Courts, X-115 pp., 1937.
111. Rainer, Rev. Eligius George, C.SS.R., J.C.D., Suspension of Clerics, XVII-249 pp., 1937.
112. Reilly, Rev. Thomas F., C.SS.R., J.C.D., Visitation of Religious, VI-195 pp., 1938.
113. Moriarity, Rev. Francis E., C.SS.R., J.C.D., The Extraordinary Absolution from Censures, XV-334 pp., 1938.
114. Connolly, Rev. Nicholas P., J.C.D., The Canonical Erection of Parishes, X-132 pp., 1938.
115. Donovan, Rev. James Joseph, J.C.D., The Pastor's Obligation in Prenuptial Investigation, XII-322 pp., 1938.
116. Harrigan, Rev. Robert J., M.A., S.T.B., J.C.D., The Radical Sanation of Invalid Marriages, VIII-208 pp., 1938.
117. Boffa, Rev. Conrad Humbert, J.C.D., Canonical Provisions for Catholic Schools, VII-211 pp., 1939.
118. Parsons, Rev. Anscar John, O.M.Cap., J.C.D., Canonical Elections, XII-236 pp., 1939.
119. Reilly, Rev. Edward Michael, A.B., J.C.D., The General Norms of Dispensation, XII-156 pp., 1939.
120. Ryan, Rev. Gerald Aloysius, A.B., J.C.D., Principles of Episcopal Jurisdiction, XII-172 pp., 1939.
121. Burton, Rev. Francis James, C.S.C., A.B., J.C.D., A Commentary on Canon 1125, X-222 pp., 1940.
122. Miaskiewicz, Rev. Francis Sigismund, J.C.D., Supplied Jurisdiction According to Canon 209, XII-340 pp., 1940.
123. Rice, Rev. Patrick William, A.B., J.C.D., Proof of Death in Prenuptial Investigation, VIII-156 pp., 1940.
124. Anglin, Rev. Thomas Francis, M.S., J.C.D., The Eucharistic Fast, VIII-183 pp., 1941.
125. Coleman, Rev. John Jerome, J.C.D., The Minister of Confirmation, VI-153 pp., 1941.
126. Downs, Rev. John Emmanuel, A.B., J.C.D., The Concept of Clerical Immunity, XI-163 pp., 1941.
127. Esswein, Rev. Anthony Albert, J.C.D., Extrajudicial Penal Powers of Ecclesiastical Superiors, X-144 pp., 1941.
128. Farrell, Rev. Benjamin Francis, M.A., S.T.L., J.C.D., The Rights and Duties of the Local Ordinary Regarding Congregations of Women Religious of Pontifical Approval, V-195 pp., 1941.
129. Feeney, Rev. Thomas John, A.B., S.T.L., J.C.D., Restitutio in Integrum, VI-169 pp., 1941.
130. Findlay, Rev. Stephen William, O.S.B., A.B., J.C.D., Canonical

Norms Governing the Deposition and Degradation of Clerics, XVII-279 pp., 1941.

131. GOODWINE, REV. JOHN, A.B., S.T.L., J.C.D., The Right of the Church to Acquire Property, VIII-119 pp., 1941.

132. HESTON, REV. EDWARD LOUIS, C.S.C., Ph.D., S.T.D., J.C.D., The Alienation of Church Property in the United States, XII-222 pp., 1941.

133. HOGAN, REV. JAMES JOHN, A.B., S.T.L., J.C.D., Judicial Advocates and Procurators, XIII-200 pp., 1941.

134. KEALY, REV. THOMAS M., A.B., Litt.B., J.C.D., Dowry of Women Religious, IX-152 pp., 1941.

135. KEENE, REV. MICHAEL JAMES, O.S.B., J.C.D., Religious Ordinaries and Canon 198, V-164 pp., 1942.

136. KERIN, REV. CHARLES A., S.S., M.A., S.T.B., J.C.D., The Privation of Christian Burial, XVI-279 pp., 1941.

137. LOUIS, REV. WILLIAM FRANCIS, M.A., J.C.D., Diocesan Archives, X-101 pp., 1941.

138. McDEVITT, REV. GILBERT JOSEPH, A.B., J.C.D., Legitimacy and Legitimation, X-247 pp., 1941.

139. McDONOUGH, REV. THOMAS JOSEPH, A.B., J.C.D., Apostolic Administrators, X-217 pp., 1941.

140. MEIER, REV. CARL ANTHONY, A.B., J.C.D., Penal Administrative Pro-cedure Against Negligent Pastors, XI-240 pp., 1941.

141. SCHMIDT, REV. JOHN ROGG, A.B., J.C.D., The Principles of Authentic Interpretation in Canon 17 of the Code of Canon Law, XII-331 pp., 1941.

142. SLAFKOSKY, REV. ANDREW LEONARD, A.B., J.C.D., The Canonical Episcopal Visitation of the Diocese, X-197 pp., 1941.

143. SWABODA, REV. INNOCENT ROBERT, O.F.M., J.C.D., Ignorance in Relation to the Imputability of Delicts, IX-271 pp., 1941.

144. DUBÉ, REV. ARTHUR JOSEPH, A. B., J.C.D., The General Principles for the Reckoning of Time in Canon Law, VIII-299 pp., 1941.

145. McBRIDE, REV. JAMES T., A.B., J.C.D., Incardination and Excardination of Seculars, XX-585 pp., 1941.

146 KRÓL, REV. JOHN T., J.C.D., The Defendant in Ecclesiastical Trials, XII-207 pp., 1942.

147. COMYNS, REV. JOSEPH J., C.SS.R., A.B., J.C.D., Papal and Episcopal Administration of Church Property, XIV-155 pp., 1942.

148. BARRY, REV. GARRETT FRANCIS, O.M.I., J.C.D., Violation of the Cloister, XII-260 pp., 1942.

149. BOLDUC, REV. GATIEN, C.S.V., A.B., S.T.L., J.C.D., Les Études dans les Religions Cléricales, VIII-155 pp., 1942.

150. BOYLE, REV. DAVID JOHN, M.A., J.C.D., The Juridic Effects of Moral Certitude on Pre-Nuptial Guarantees, XII-188 pp., 1942.

151. CANAVAN, REV. WALTER JOSEPH, M.A., Litt.D., J.C.D., The Profes-sion of Faith, XII-143 pp., 1942.

152. DESROCHERS, REV. BRUNO, A.B., Ph.L., S.T.B., J.C.D., Le Premier Concile Plénier de Québéc et le Code de Droit Canonique, XIV–186 pp., 1942.
153. DILLON, REV. ROBERT EDWARD, A.B., J.C.D., Common Law Marriage, X-148 pp., 1942.
154. DODWELL, REV. EDWARD JOHN, Ph.D., S.T.B., J.C.D., The Time and Place for the Celebration of Marriage, X-156 pp., 1942.
155. DONNELLAN, REV. THOMAS ANDREW, A.B., J.C.D., The Obligation of the Missa pro Populo, VII-131 pp., 1942.
156. ELTZ, REV. LOUIS ANTHONY, A.B., J.C.D., Cooperation in Crime, XII-208 pp., 1942.
157. GASS, REV. SYLVESTER FRANCIS, M.A., J.C.D., Ecclesiastical Pensions, XI-206 pp., 1942.
158. GUINIVEN, REV. JOHN JOSEPH, C.SS.R., J.C.D., The Precept of Hearing Mass, XIV-188 pp., 1942.
159. GLUCZYNSKI, REV. JOHN THEOPHILUS, J.C.D., The Desecration and Violation of Churches, X-126 pp., 1942.
160. HAMMILL, REV. JOHN LEO, M.A., J.C.D., The Obligations of the Traveler According to Canon 14, VIII-204 pp., 1942.
161. HAYDT, REV. JOHN JOSEPH, A.B., J.C.D., Reserved Benefices, XI-148 pp., 1942.
162. HUSER, REV. ROGER JOHN, O.F.M., A.B., J.C.D., The Crime of Abortion in Canon Law, XII-187 pp., 1942.
163. KEARNEY, REV. FRANCIS PATRICK, A.B., S.T.L., J.C.D., The Principles of Canon 1127, X-162 pp., 1942.
164. LINAHEN, REV. LEO JAMES, S.T.L., J.C.D., De Absolutione Complicis In Peccato Turpi, 114 pp., 1942.
165. McCLOSKEY, REV. JOSEPH ALOYSIUS, A.B., J.C.D., The Subject of Ecclesiastical Law According to Canon 12, XVII-246 pp., 1942.
166. O'NEILL, REV. FRANCIS JOSEPH, C.SS.R., J.C.D., The Dismissal of Religious in Temporary Vows, XIII-220 pp., 1942.
167. PRINCE, REV. JOHN EDWARD, A.B., S.T.B., J.C.D., The Diocesan Chancellor, X-136 pp., 1942.
168. RIESNER, REV. ALBERT JOSEPH, C.SS.R., J.C.D., Apostates and Fugitives from Religious Institutes, IX-168 pp., 1942.
169. STENGER, REV. JOSEPH BERNARD, J.C.D., The Mortgaging of Church Property, 186 pp., 1942.
170. WALDRON, REV. JOSEPH FRANCIS, A.B., J.C.D., The Minister of Baptism, XII-197 pp., 1942.
171. WILLETT, REV. ROBERT ALBERT, J.C.D., The Probative Value of Documents in Ecclesiastical Trials, X-124 pp., 1942.
172. WOEBER, REV. EDWARD MARTIN, M.A., J.C.D., The Interpellations, XII-161 pp., 1942.
173. BENKO, REV. MATTHEW ALOYSIUS, O.S.B., M.A., J.C.D., The Abbot *Nullius*, XVI-148 pp., 1943.

174. CHRIST, REV. JOSEPH JAMES, M.A., S.T.L., J.C.D., Dispensation from Vindicative Penalties, XIV-285 pp., 1943.
175. CLANCY, REV. PATRICK M. J., O.P., A.B., S.T.Lr., J.C.D., The Local Religious Superior, X-229 pp., 1943.
176. CLARKE, REV. THOMAS JAMES, J.C.D., Parish Societies, XII-147 pp., 1943.
177. CONNOLLY, REV. JOHN PATRICK, S.T.L., J.C.D., Synodal Examiners and Parish Priest Consultors, X-223 pp., 1943.
178. DRUMM, REV. WILLIAM MARTIN, A.B., J.C.D., Hospital Chaplains, XII-175 pp., 1943.
179. FLANAGAN, REV. BERNARD JOSEPH, A.B., S.T.L., J.C.D., The Canonical Erection of Religious Houses, X-147 pp., 1943.
180. KELLEHER, REV. STEPHEN JOSEPH, A.B., S.T.B., J.C.D., Discussions with Non-Catholics: Canonical Legislation, X-93 pp., 1943.
181. LEWIS, REV. GORDIAN, C.P., J.C.D., Chapters in Religious Institutes, XII-169 pp., 1943.
182. MARX, REV. ADOLPH, J.C.D., The Declaration of Nullity of Marriages Contracted Outside the Church, X-151 pp., 1943.
183. MATULENAS, REV. RAYMOND ANTHONY, O.S.B., A.B., J.C.D., Communication, a Source of Privileges, XII-225 pp., 1943.
184. O'LEARY, REV. CHARLES GERARD, C.SS.R., J.C.D., Religious Dismissed After Perpetual Profession, X-213 pp., 1943.
185. POWER, REV. CORNELIUS MICHAEL, J.C.D., The Blessing of Cemeteries, XII-231 pp., 1943.
186. SHUHLER, REV. RALPH VINCENT, O.S.A., J.C.D., Privileges of Regulars to Absolve and Dispense, XII-195 pp., 1943.
187. ZIOLKOWSKI, REV. THADDEUS STANISLAUS, A.B., J.C.D., The Consecration and Blessing of Churches, XII-151 pp., 1943.
188. HENEGHAN, REV. JOHN JOSEPH, S.T.D., J.C.D., The Marriages of Unworthy Catholics: Canons 1065 and 1066, XVI-213 pp., 1944.
189. CARROLL, REV. COLEMAN FRANCIS, M.A., S.T.L., J.C.L., Charitable Institutions.
190. CIESLUK, REV. JOSEPH EDWARD, Ph.B., S.T.L., J.C.D., National Parishes in the United States, VI-178 pp., 1944.
191. COBURN, REV. VINCENT PAUL, A.B., J.C.D., Marriages of Conscience, XII-172 pp., 1944.
192. CONNORS, REV. CHARLES PAUL, C.S.Sp., A.B., J.C.D., Extra-Judicial Procurators in the Code of Canon Law, X-94 pp., 1944.
193. COYLE, REV. PAUL RAYMOND, A.B., J.C.D., Judicial Exceptions, X-142 pp., 1944.
194. FAIR, REV. BARTHOLOMEW FRANCIS, A.B., S.T.L., J.C.D., The Impediment of Abduction, XII-122 pp., 1944.
195. GALLAGHER, REV. THOMAS RAPHAEL, O.P., A.B., S.T.Lr., J.C.D., The Examination of the Qualities of the Ordinand, X-166 pp., 1944.
196. GANNON, REV. JOHN MARK, S.T.L., J.C.D., The Interstices Required for the Promotion to Orders, XII-100 pp., 1944.

197. GOLDSMITH, REV. J. WILLIAM, B.C.S., S.T.L., J.C.D., The Competence of Church and State over Marriage—Disputed Points, X-128 pp., 1944.
198. GOODWINE, REV. JOSEPH GERARD, A.B., S.T.D., J.C.D., The Reception of Converts, XIV-326 pp., 1944.
199. KOWALSKI, REV. ROMUALD EUGENE, O.F.M., A.B., J.C.D., Sustenance of Religious Houses of Regulars, X-174 pp., 1944.
200. McCOY, REV. ALAN EDWARD, O.F.M., J.C.D., Force and Fear in Relation to Delictual Imputability and Penal Responsibility, XII-160 pp., 1944.
201. McDEVITT, REV. VINCENT JOHN, Ph.B., S.T.L., J.C.L., Perjury.
202. MARTIN, REV. THOMAS OWEN, Ph.D., S.T.D., J.C.D., Adverse Possession, Prescription and Limitation of Actions: The Canonical "Praescriptio," XX-208 pp., 1944.
203. MIKLOSOVIC, REV. PAUL JOHN, A.B., J.C.L., Attempted Marriages and Their Consequent Juridic Effects.
204. MUNDY, REV. THOMAS MAURICE, A.B., S.T.L., J.C.D., The Union of Parishes, X—164 pp., 1944.
205. O'DEA, REV. JOHN COYLE, A.B., J.C.D., The Matrimonial Impediment of Nonage, VIII-126 pp., 1944.
206. OLALIA, REV. ALEXANDER AYSON, S.T.L., J.C.D., A Comparative Study of the Christian Constitution of States and the Constitution of the Philippine Commonwealth, XII—136 pp., 1944.
207. POISSON, REV. PIERRE-MARIE, C.S.C., A.B., Ph.L., Th.L., J.C.L., Droits Patrimoniaux des Maisons et des Églises Religieuses.
208. STADALNIKAS, REV. CASIMIR JOSEPH, M.I.C., J.C.D., Reservation of Censures, X-141 pp., 1944.
209. SULLIVAN, REV. EUGENE HENRY, S.T.L., J.C.D., Proof of the Reception of the Sacraments, X—165 pp., 1944.
210. VAUGHAN, REV. WILLIAM EDWARD, J.C.D., Constitutions for Diocesan Courts, X-210 pp., 1944.
211. PARO, REV. GINO, S.T.D., J.C.L., The Right of Apostolic Legation.
212. BALZER, REV. RALPH FRANCIS, C.P., J.C.D., The Computation of Time in a Canonical Novitiate, X—227 pp., 1945.
213. DOUGHERTY, REV. JOHN WHELAN, A.B., S.T.L., J.C.D., De Inquisitione Speciali, XII—195 pp., 1945.
214. DZIOB, REV. MICHAEL WALTER, J.C.D., The Sacred Congregation for the Oriental Church, XII—181 pp., 1945.
215. EIDENSCHINK, REV. JOHN ALBERT, O.S.B., B.A., J.C.D, The Election of Bishops in the Letters of Pope Gregory the Great, VII—200 pp., 1945.
216. GILL, REV. NICHOLAS, C.P., J.C.D., The Spiritual Prefect in Clerical Religious Houses of Study, X—140 pp., 1945.
217. HYNES, REV. HARRY GERARD, S.T.L., J.C.D., The Privileges of Cardinals, XII-183 pp., 1945.
218. McDEVITT, REV. GERALD VINCENT, S.T.L., J.C.D., The Renunciation of an Ecclesiastical Office, XIV—179 pp., 1945.

219. Manning, Rev. Joseph Leroy, J.C.D., The Free Conferral of Offices, VIII—116 pp., 1945.
220. **Meyer, Rev. Louis G., O.S.B., A.B., S.T.B., J.C.D., Alms-Gathering** by Religious, XII—163 pp., 1945.
221. O'Donnell, Rev. Cletus Francis, M.A., J.C.D., The Marriage of Minors, XII—268 pp., 1945.
222. **Prunskis, Rev. Joseph, J.C.D., Comparative Law, Ecclesiastical and Civil, in Lithuanian Concordat, X—161 pp., 1945.**
223. **Sweeney, Rev. Francis Patrick, C.SS.R., J.C.D., The Reduction of Clerics to the Lay State, X—199 pp., 1945.**
224. Vogelpohl, Rev. Henry John, J.C.D., The Simple Impediments to Holy Orders, XVI—190 pp., 1945.
225. Brockhaus, Rev. Thomas Aquinas, O.S.B., A.B., J.C.D., Religious who Are Known as *Conversi,* X—127 pp., 1945.
226. Griese, Rev. N. Orville, S.T.D., J.C.D., The Marriage Contract and the Procreation of Offspring, XVI-224 pp., 1946.
227. Boudreaux, Rev. Warren Louis, J.C.D., The *"ab acatholicis nati"* of Canon 1099, § 2, XII-110 pp., 1946.
228. Bowe, Rev. Thomas Joseph, A.B., J.C.D., Religious Superioresses, VIII-206 pp., 1946.
229. Diederichs, Rev. Michael Ferdinand, S.C.J., J.C.D., The Jurisdiction of the Latin Ordinaries over their Oriental Subjects, XIV-153 pp., 1946.
230. Dingman, Rev. Maurice John, A.B., S.T.L., J.C.L., The Plaintiff in Contentious Trials.
231. Frison, Rev. Basil, C.M.F., M.Mus., J.C.D., The Retroactivity of Law, X-221 pp., 1946.
232. Galvin, Rev. William Anthony, M.A., J.C.D., The Administrative Transfer of Pastors, XII-288 pp., 1946.
233. Goracy, Rev. Joseph C., J.C.L., The Diriment Matrimonial Impediment of Major Orders.
234. Hale, Rev. Joseph Francis, M.A., S.T.L., J.C.L., The Pastor of Burial.
235. Henry, Rev. Joseph Arthur, A.B., J.C.D., The Mass and Holy Communion: Inter-Ritual Law, XII-138 pp., 1946.
236. Linenberger, Rev. Herbert, C.PP.S., J.C.L., The False Denunciation of an Innocent Confessor.
237. Lowry, Rev. James Martin, A.B., J.C.D., Dispensation from Private Vows, XII-266 pp., 1946.
238. Lynch, Rev. George Edward, A.B., S.T.L., J.C.D., Coadjutors and Auxiliaries of Bishops, X-107 pp., 1947.
239. Lynch, Rev. Timothy, M.S.SS.T., J.C.D., Contracts between Bishops and Religious Congregations, XIV-232 pp., 1946.
240. McClunn, Rev. Justin David, A.B., S.T.L., J.C.D., Administrative Recourse, VII-142 pp., 1946.

241. Lohmuller, Rev. Martin Nicholas, A.B., J.C.D., The Promulgation of Law, XII-140 pp., 1947.
242. McGrath, Rev. James, A.B., J.C.D., The Privilege of the Canon, XII-156 pp., 1946.
243. Marbach, Rev. Joseph Francis, A.B., J.C.D., Marriage Legislation for the Catholics of the Oriental Rites in the United States and Canada, XIV-314 pp., 1946.
244. Shimkus, Rev. Bernard Aloysius, A.B., J.C.L., The Determination and Transfer of Rite.
245. Smith, Rev. Vincent Michael, A.B., S.T.L., J.C.L., Ignorance Affecting Matrimonial Consent.
246. Wachtrle, Rev. Paul Anthony, A.B., J.C.L., The Baptism of the Children of Non-Catholics.
247. Crotty, Rev. Matthew Michael, J.C.D., The Recipient of First Holy Communion, X-142 pp., 1947.
248. Eagleton, Rev. George, J.C.L., The Quinquennial Faculties, Formula IV.
249. Gibbons, Rev. Marion Leo, C.M., J.C.D., Domicile of the Wife Unlawfully Separated from Her Husband, XIV-171 pp., 1947.
250. Kelly, Rev. Bernard Matthew, S.T.L., J.C.D., The Functions Reserved to Pastors, X-150 pp., 1947.
251. Kilcullen, Rev. Thomas John, LL.M., J.C.D., The Collegiate Moral Person as Party Litigant, X-150 pp., 1947.
252. Lafontaine, Rev. Germain Joseph, W.F., J.C.L., Relations Canoniques entre le Missionaire et Ses Superieurs.
253. Lane, Rev. Loras Thomas, J.C.L., Matrimonial Procedure in Ordinary Court of Second Instance.
254. Lover, Rev. James Francis, C.Ss.R., J.C.D., The Master of Novices, X-168 pp., 1947.
255. McNicholas, Rev. Timothy Joseph, J.C.D., The *Septimae Manus* Witness, XII—133 pp., 1947 (printed 1949).
256. Marositz, Rev. Joseph John, M.S.C., J.C.D., Obligations and Privileges of Religious Promoted to the Episcopal or Cardinalitial Dignities, XII-180 pp. 1947.
257. Murphy, Rev. Francis Joseph, J.C.D., Legislative Powers of the Provincial Council, XII-158 pp., 1947.
258. O'Brien, Rev. Romaeus William, O.Carm., J.C.D., The Provincial Superior in Religious Orders of Men, X-294 pp., 1947.
259. Pfaller, Rev. Benedict Anthony, O.S.B., J.C.L., *The ipso facto* Effected Dismissal of Religious.
260. Popek, Rev. Alphonse Sylvester, J.C.D., The Rights and Obligations of Metropolitans, XVIII-460 pp., 1947.
261. Ristuccia, Rev. Bernard Joseph, C.M., J.C.L., Quasi-Religious.
262. Sonntag, Rev. Nathaniel Louis, O.F.M.Cap., J.C.D., Censorship of Special Classes of Books, XII-147 pp., 1947.

263. STADLER, REV. JOSEPH NICHOLAS, J.C.L., Frequent Holy Communion.
264. SZAL, REV. IGNATIUS JOSEPH, J.C.D., The Communication of Catholics with Schismatics, XII-217 pp., 1947.
265. WAGNER, REV. URBAN STANLEY, O.F.M.Conv., J.C.D., Parochial Substitute Vicars and Supplying Priests, IX-126 pp., 1947.
266. QUINN, REV. JOSEPH, M.A., J.C.L., Documents Required for the Reception of Orders.
267. BENNINGTON, REV. JAMES CLEMENT, A.B., J.C.L., The Recipient of Confirmation.
268. BLAHER, REV. DAMIAN JOSEPH, O.F.M., A.B., J.C.D., The Ordinary Processes in Causes of Beautification and Canonization, XVI—290 pp., 1948 (printed 1949).
269. CLUNE, REV. ROBERT BELL, B.A., J.C.D., The Judicial Interrogation of the Parties, XII—142 pp., 1948.
270. COURTEMANCHE, REV. BASIL F., B.A., J.C.D., The Total Simulation of Matrimonial Consent, XX—120 pp., 1948.
271. DLOUHY, REV. MAUR JOHN, O.S.B., A.B., J.C.L., The Ordination of Exempt Religious.
272. DONOVAN, REV. JOHN THOMAS, PH.B., S.T.L., J.C.L., The Clerical Obligations of Canons 138 and 140.
273. FREKING, REV. FREDERICK W., A.B., S.T.B., J.C.D., The Canonical Installation of Pastors, XII—210 pp., 1948.
274. FULTON, REV. THOMAS B., J.C.D., Prenuptial Investigation, XII—190 pp., 1948.
275. GODLEY, REV. JAMES P., J.C.D., Time and Place for the Celebration of Mass, X—206 pp., 1948 (printed 1949).
276. KANE, REV. THOMAS A., A.B., B.S., J.C.D., The Jurisdiction of the Patriarchs of the Major Sees in Antiquity and in the Middle Ages, XII—153 pp., 1948 (printed 1949).
277. KENNEDY, REV. ANDREW A., J.C.L., The Annual Pastoral Report to the Local Ordinary.
278. KONRAD, REV. JOSEPH GEORGE, J.C.D., Transfer of Religious to Another Community, VIII—284 pp., 1948 (printed 1949).
279. KRESS, REV. ALPHONSE, J.C.L., Contumacy in Ecclesiastical Trials.
280. MCCARTNEY, REV. MARCELLUS ANTHONY, O.F.M., M.A., J.C.D., Faculties of Regular Confessors, XII—164 pp., 1948 (printed 1949).
281. MCCASLIN, REV. EDWARD PATRICK, M.A., S.T.L., J.C.L., The Division of Parishes.
282. MCELROY, REV. FRANCIS J., A.B., J.C.L., The Privileges of Bishops.
283. QUINN, REV. STEPHEN, M.S.SS.T., J.C.L., Relation of the Local Ordinary to Religious of Diocesan Approval.
284. SCHNEIDER, REV. EDELHARD LOUIS, S.D.S., M.A., J.C.L., The Status of Secularized Ex-Religious Clerics.
285. THOMPSON, REV. CHESTER J., A.B., J.C.L., The Simple Removal from Office.

286. O'BRIEN, REV. KENNETH R., A.B., J.C.D., The Nature of Support of Diocesan Priests in the United States, XVI-162 pp., 1949.
287. METZ, REV. JOHN E., S.T.L., J.C.D., The Recording Judge in the Ecclesiastical Collegiate Tribunal, X-130 pp., 1949.
288. REINHARDT, REV. MARION J., S.T.L., J.C.D., The Rogatory Commission, XIII—182 pp., 1949.
289. ORTEGA UHIUK, REV. JUAN, S.J., J.C.L., De Delicto Sollicitationis.
290. CASEY, REV. JAMES V., J.C.D., A Study of Canon 2222 § 1, XII-127 pp., 1949.
291. ALLGEIER, REV. JOSEPH L., J.C.D., The Canonical Obligation of Preaching in Parish Churches, X—115 pp., 1949 (printed 1950).
292. CAHILL, REV. DANIEL R., J.C.D., The Custody of the Holy Eucharist, XVI—178 pp., 1949 (printed 1950).
293. CARR, REV. AIDEN, O.F.M. Conv., S.T.D., J.C.L., Vocation to the Priesthood: Its Canonical Concept.
294. KNOPKE, REV. ROCH F., O.F.M., J.C.D., Reverential Fear in Matrimonial Cases in Asiatic Countries: Rota Cases, XII—112 pp., 1949.
295. LAVELLE, REV. HOWARD D., J.C.D., The Obligation of Holding Sacred Missions in Parishes, XVI—142 pp., 1949.
296. MICKELLS, REV. ANTHONY B., J.C.L., The Constitutive Elements of Parishes.
297. NOONE, REV. JOHN J., J.C.D., Nullity in Judicial Acts, X—147 pp., 1949 (printed 1950).
298. SHEEHAN, REV. DANIEL E., J.C.L., The Minister of Holy Communion.
299. STATKUS, REV. FRANCIS J., J.C.L., The Minister of the Last Sacraments.
300. COOK, REV. JOHN P., J.C.D., Ecclesiastical Communities and Their Ability to Induce Legal Customs, XII—152 pp., 1949 (printed 1950).
301. FAZZALARO, REV. FRANCIS J., J.C.D., The Place for the Hearing of Confessions, X—150 pp., 1949 (printed 1950).
302. HANNAN, REV. PHILIP M., J.C.D., The Canonical Concept of *congrua sustentatio* for the Secular Clergy, XII—237 pp., 1949 (printed 1950).
303. QUINN, REV. HUGH G., S.T.L., J.C.L., The Particular Penal Precept.
304. GALLAGHER, REV. JOHN F., J.C.L., The Matrimonial Impediment of Public Propriety.
305. WELSH, REV. THOMAS J., J.C.L., The Use of the Portable Altar.
306. WATERS, REV. JOSEPH L., S.S.J., J.C.L., The Probation in Societies of Quasi-Religious.
307. REGAN, REV. MICHAEL J., J.C.L., Canon 16.
308. BYRNE, REV. HARRY J., J.C.L., Investment of Church Funds.
309. GALLAGHER, REV. THOMAS V., J.C.L., The Rejection of Judicial Witnesses and Testimony.
310. CHATHAM, REV. JOSIAH G., Ph.B., S.T.L., J.C.L., Force and Fear as Invalidating Marriage: The Element of Injustice.

311. BROWN, REV. JAMES VICTOR, O.R.S.A., J.C.L., The Invalidating Effects of Force, Fear, and Fraud upon the Canonical Novitiate.
312. DUERR, REV. CHARLES J., B.A., J.C.L., The Judicial Notary.
313. GONZALEZ, REV. FRANCISCO J., O.S.A., J.C.L., De Parocho Religioso Eiusque Superiore Locali.
314. HANNON, REV. JAMES J., J.C.L., Holy Viaticum.
315. SADLOWSKI, REV. ERWIN L., J. C. L., The Sacred Furnishings of Churches.
316. SEGO, REV. ARTHUR A., J.C.L., Dispensation from the Interpellations.
317. WATERHOUSE, REV. JOHN M., J.C.L., The Power of the Local Ordinary to Impose a Matrimonial Ban.
318. FREIN, REV. EUGENE B., J.C.L., The Discretionary Power of the Defender of the Matrimonial Bond.
319. CARTON, REV. GEORGE A., J.C.L., The Time Factor in the Gaining of Indulgences.
320. WALSH, REV. JOHN J., C.S.Sp., J.C.L., The Jurisdiction of the Inter-ritual Confessor in the United States and Canada.
321. UNTERKOEFLER, REV. ERNEST L., S.T.L., J.C.L., The Presiding Judge in Matrimonial Causes of First Instance.

www.ingramcontent.com/pod-product-compliance
Lightning Source LLC
LaVergne TN
LVHW050216080826
844660LV00012B/418

* 9 7 8 0 8 1 3 2 2 4 8 1 7 *